P9-EMR-820

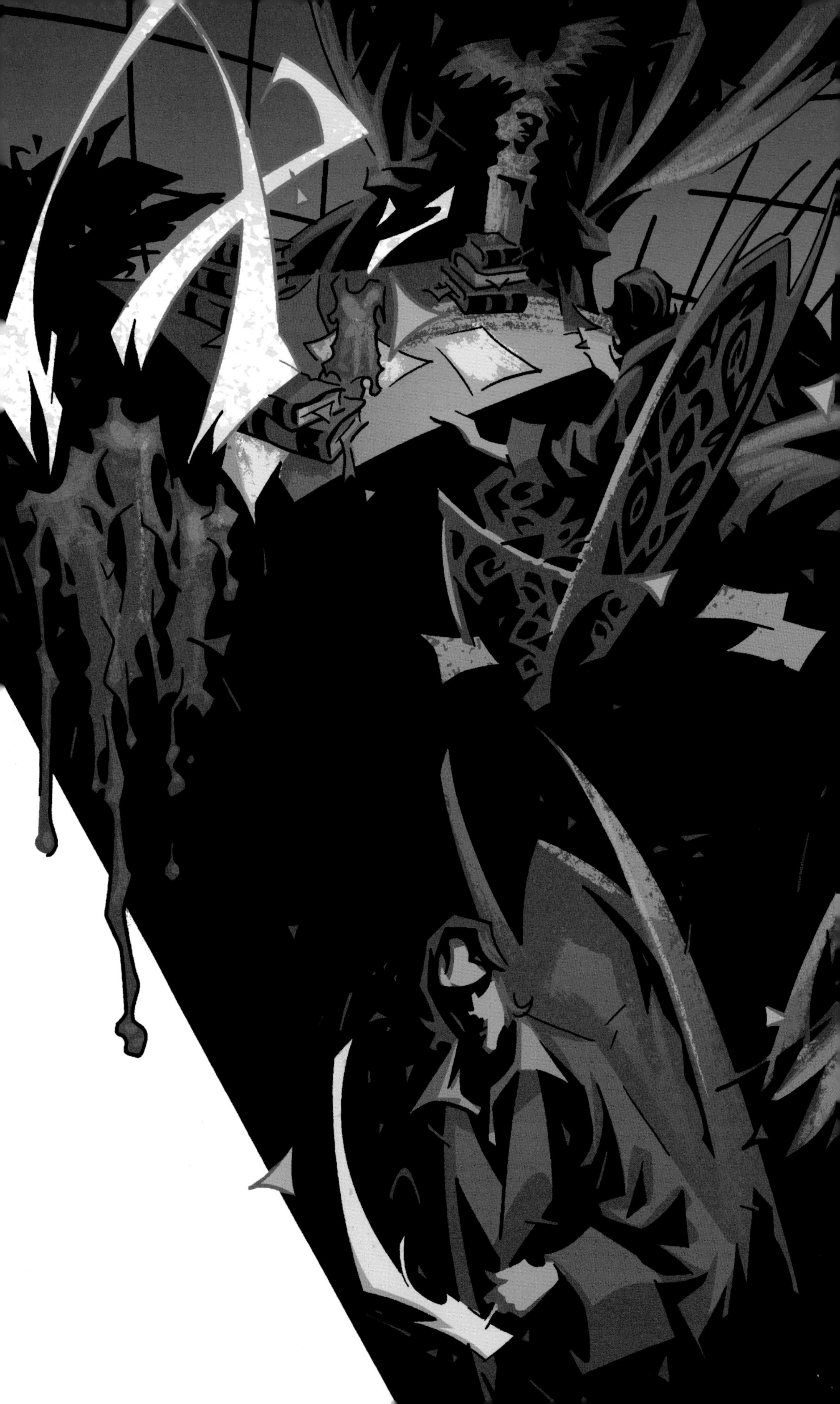

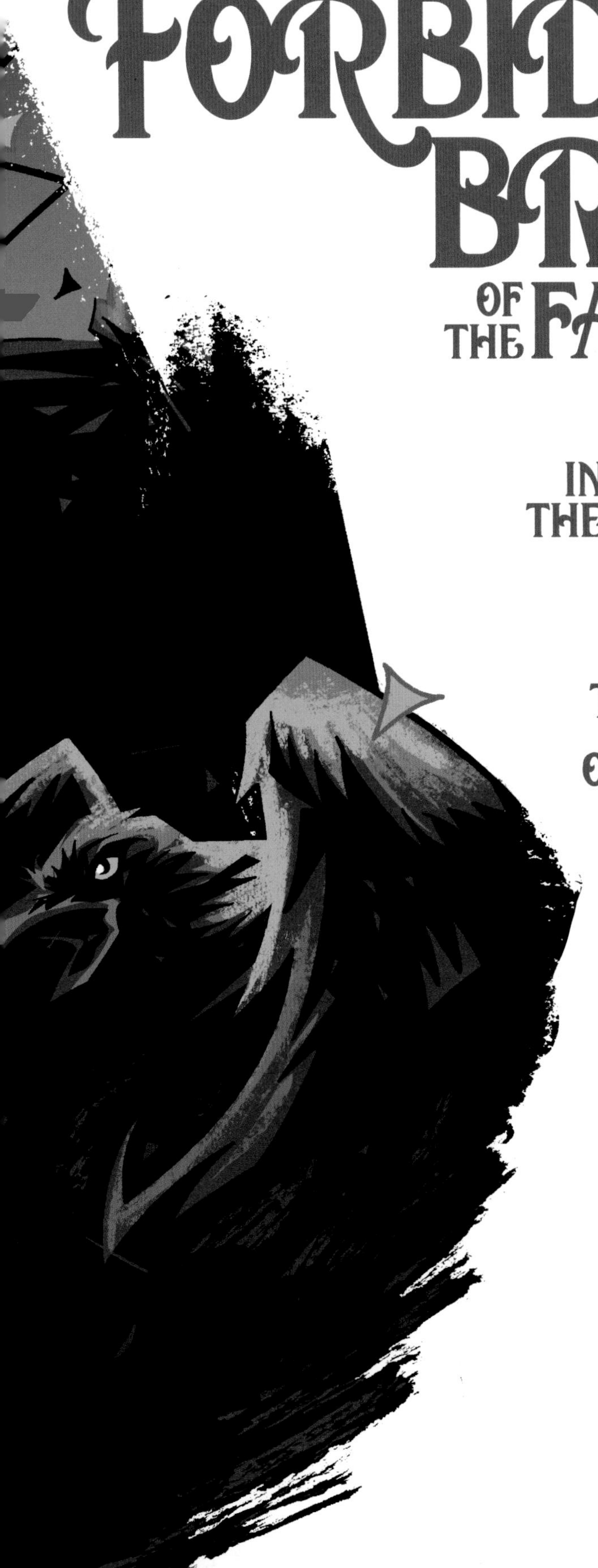

FORBIDDEN BRIDES OF THE FACELESS SLAVES IN THE SECRET HOUSE OF THE NIGHT OF DREAD DESIRE

STORY
NEIL GAIMAN

ADAPTATION AND ART
SHANE OAKLEY

COLORS
(PAGES 5, 12–14, 18–25, 32–36, 40–42)
NICK FILARDI

LETTERING
TODD KLEIN

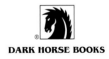

DARK HORSE BOOKS

**To Rick and Claire, for always making me feel so welcome.
To Suzanne, for mopping my brow and talking sense.
And to the memory of Mojo—the Little King of Gummidge!**
—Shane Oakley

PRESIDENT AND PUBLISHER
MIKE RICHARDSON

EDITOR
DANIEL CHABON

ASSISTANT EDITOR
CARDNER CLARK

DESIGNER
ETHAN KIMBERLING

DIGITAL ART TECHNICIAN
ALLYSON HALLER

Published by Dark Horse Books
A division of Dark Horse Comics, Inc.
10956 SE Main Street
Milwaukie, OR 97222

DarkHorse.com

To find a comic shop in your area, call the Comic Shop
Locator Service: (888) 266-4226
International Licensing: (503) 905-2377

First edition: January 2017
ISBN 978-1-50670-140-0

10 9 8 7 6 5 4 3 2
Printed in Canada

Library of Congress Cataloging-in-Publication Data
Names: Gaiman, Neil, author. | Oakley, Shane, artist. | Filardi, Nick, colorist. | Klein, Todd, letterer.
Title: Forbidden brides of the faceless slaves in the secret house of the night of dread desire / Neil Gaiman, story ; Shane Oakley, art ; Nick Filardi, colors (pages 5, 12-14, 18-25, 32-36, 40-42) ; Todd Klein, lettering.
Description: First edition. | Milwaukie, OR : Dark Horse Books, 2017.
Identifiers: LCCN 2016034856 | ISBN 9781506701400 (hardback)
Subjects: LCSH: Graphic novels. | BISAC: COMICS & GRAPHIC NOVELS / Horror. | COMICS & GRAPHIC NOVELS / Fantasy. | COMICS & GRAPHIC NOVELS / General.
Classification: LCC PN6737.G3 F67 2016 | DDC 741.5/942--dc23
LC record available at https://lccn.loc.gov/2016034856

Neil Hankerson, *Executive Vice President* · Tom Weddle, *Chief Financial Officer* · Randy Stradley, *Vice President of Publishing* · Michael Martens, *Vice President of Book Trade Sales* · Matt Parkinson, *Vice President of Marketing* · David Scroggy, *Vice President of Product Development* · Dale LaFountain, *Vice President of Information Technology* · Cara Niece, *Vice President of Production and Scheduling* · Nick McWhorter, *Vice President of Media Licensing* · Ken Lizzi, *General Counsel* · Dave Marshall, *Editor in Chief* · Davey Estrada, *Editorial Director* · Scott Allie, *Executive Senior Editor* · Chris Warner, *Senior Books Editor* · Cary Grazzini, *Director of Specialty Projects* · Lia Ribacchi, *Art Director* · Vanessa Todd, *Director of Print Purchasing* · Matt Dryer, *Director of Digital Art and Prepress* · Mark Bernardi , *Director of Digital Publishing* · Sarah Robertson, *Director of Product Sales* · Michael Gombos, *Director of International Publishing and Licensing*

SOMEWHERE IN THE NIGHT,
SOMEONE WAS WRITING.

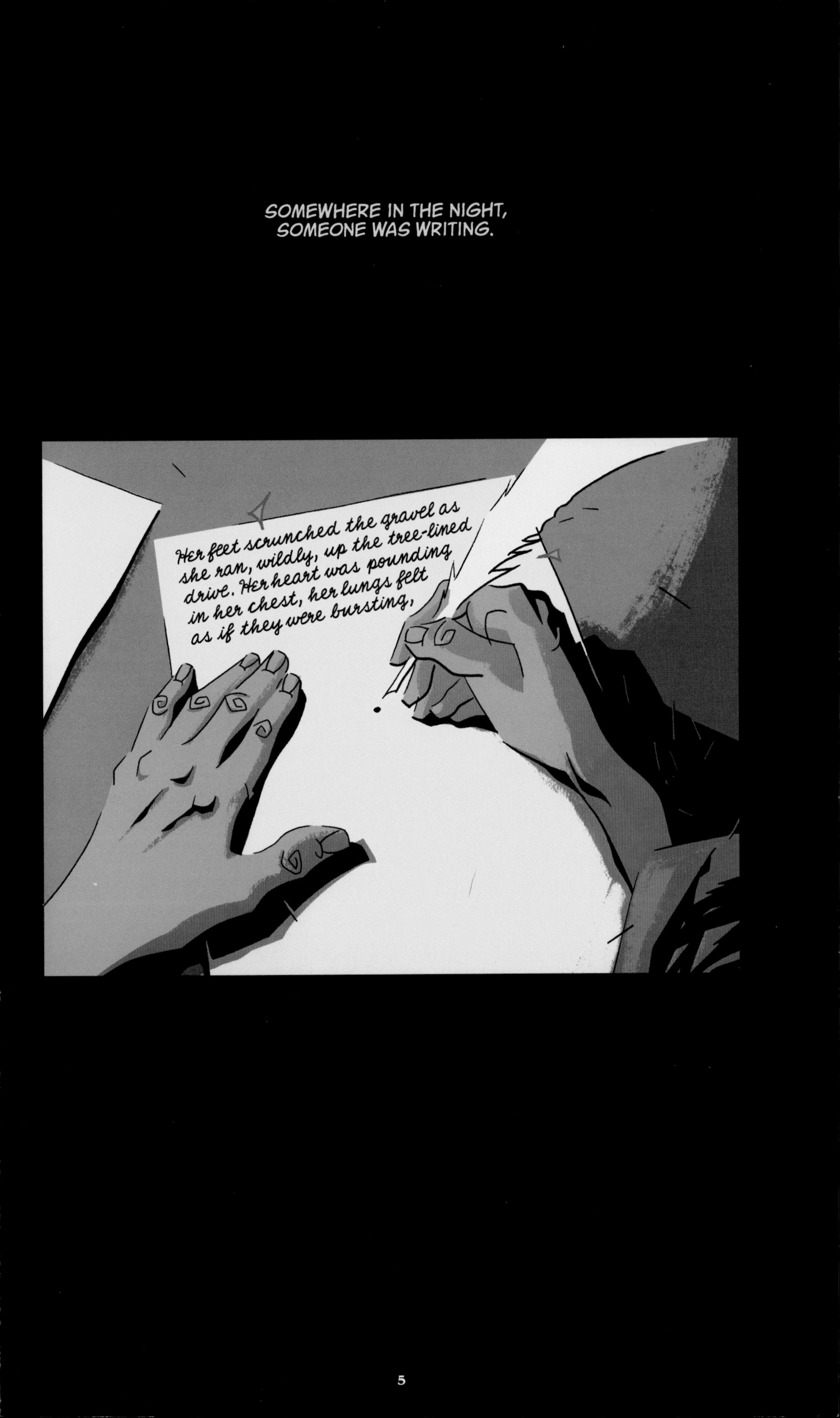
Her feet scrunched the gravel as she ran, wildly, up the tree-lined drive. Her heart was pounding in her chest, her lungs felt as if they were bursting,

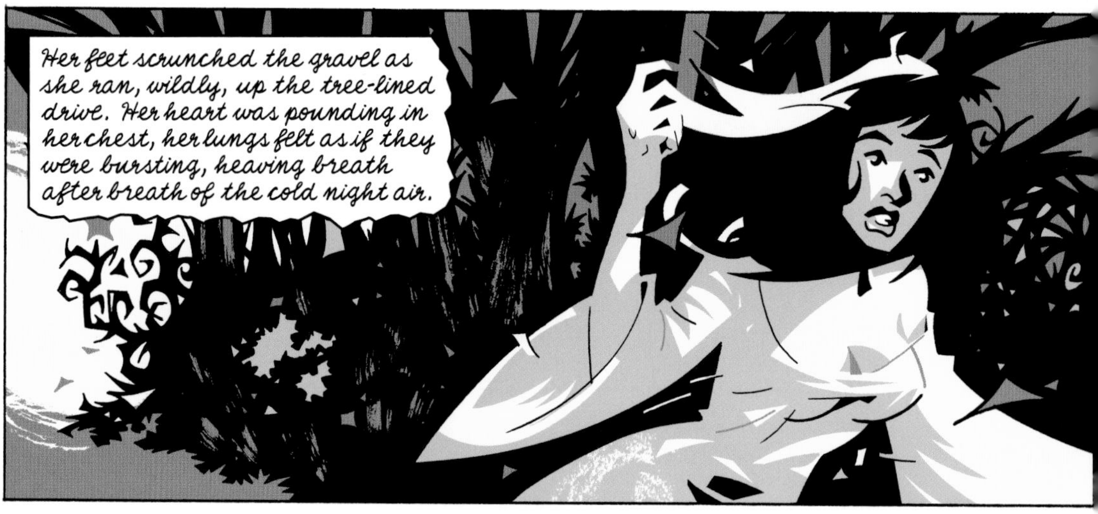
Her feet scrunched the gravel as she ran, wildly, up the tree-lined drive. Her heart was pounding in her chest, her lungs felt as if they were bursting, heaving breath after breath of the cold night air.

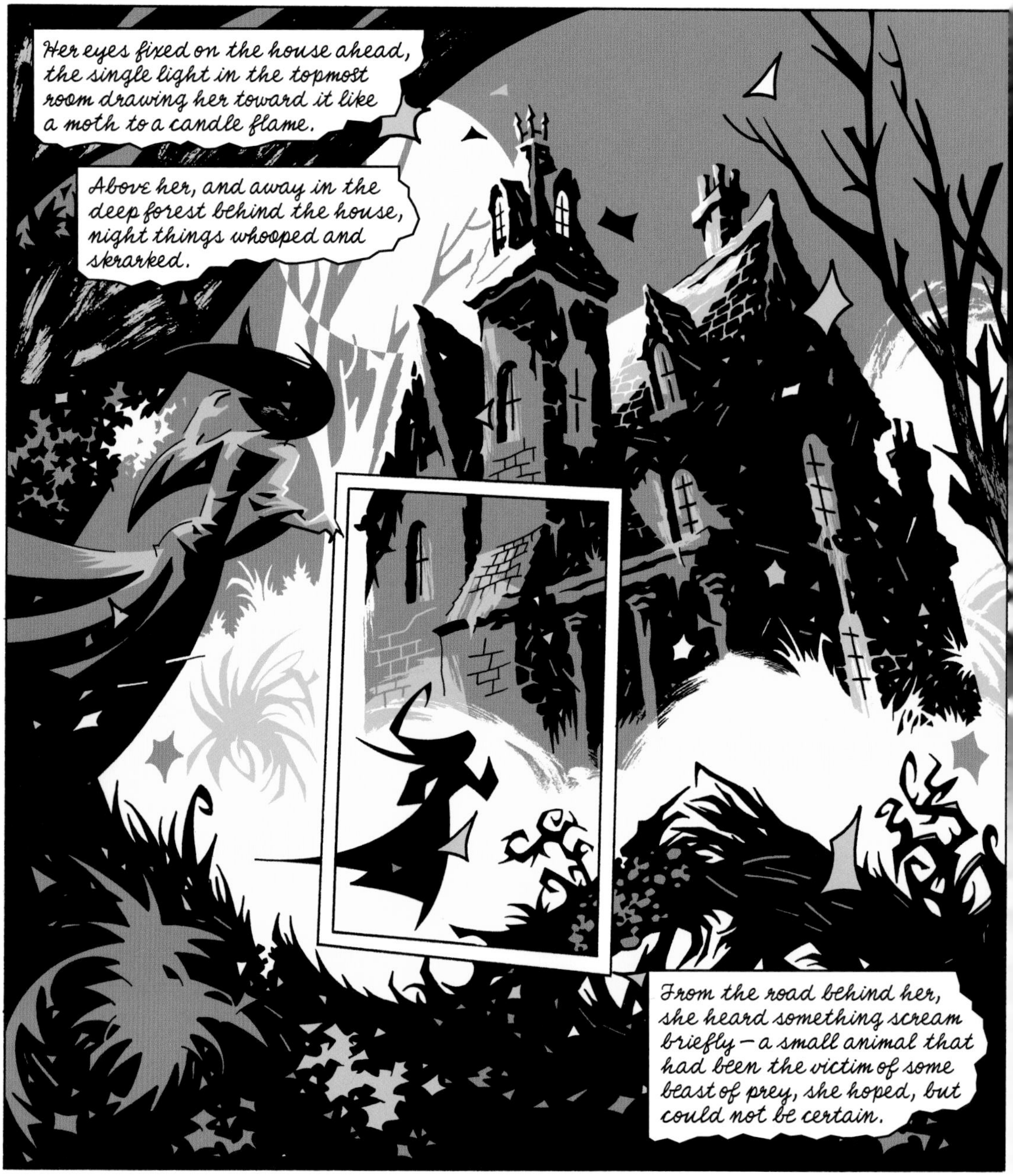
Her eyes fixed on the house ahead, the single light in the topmost room drawing her toward it like a moth to a candle flame.
Above her, and away in the deep forest behind the house, night things whooped and skrarked.
From the road behind her, she heard something scream briefly—a small animal that had been the victim of some beast of prey, she hoped, but could not be certain.

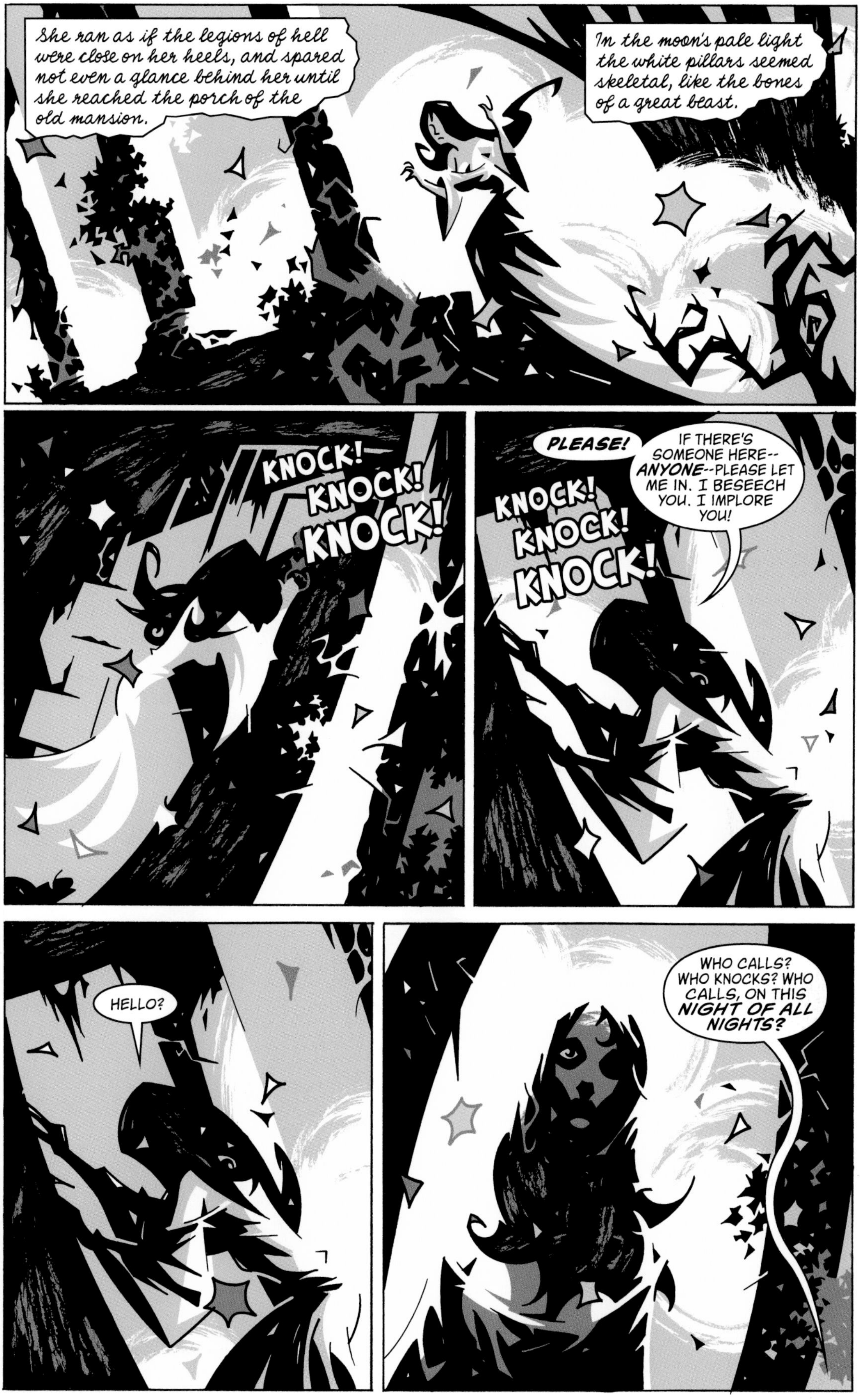
She ran as if the legions of hell were close on her heels, and spared not even a glance behind her until she reached the porch of the old mansion.
In the moon's pale light the white pillars seemed skeletal, like the bones of a great beast.
KNOCK! KNOCK! KNOCK!
PLEASE!
IF THERE'S SOMEONE HERE-- ANYONE--PLEASE LET ME IN. I BESEECH YOU. I IMPLORE YOU!
KNOCK! KNOCK! KNOCK!
HELLO?
WHO CALLS? WHO KNOCKS? WHO CALLS, ON THIS NIGHT OF ALL NIGHTS?

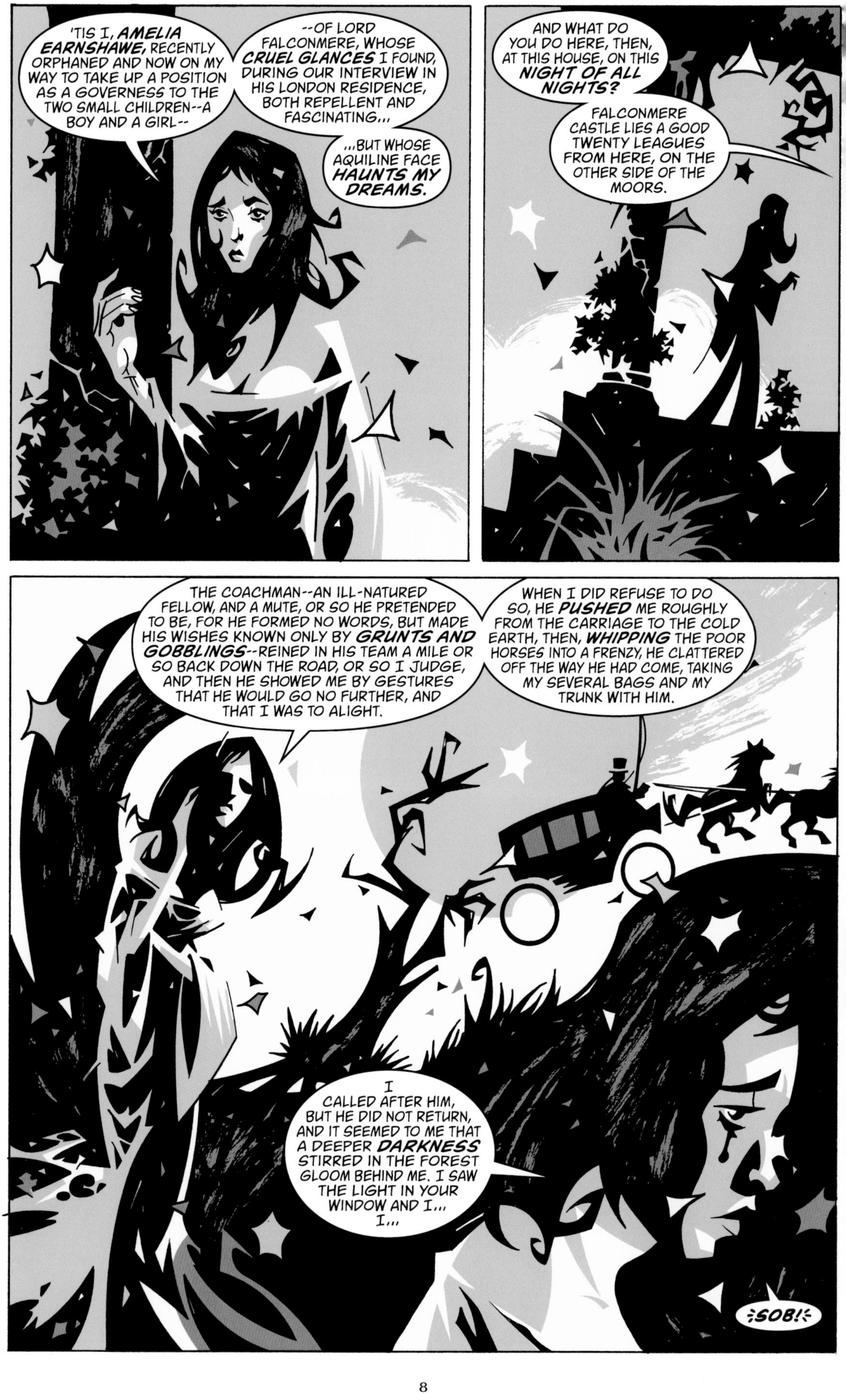
'TIS I, AMELIA EARNSHAWE, RECENTLY ORPHANED AND NOW ON MY WAY TO TAKE UP A POSITION AS A GOVERNESS TO THE TWO SMALL CHILDREN--A BOY AND A GIRL--
--OF LORD FALCONMERE, WHOSE CRUEL GLANCES I FOUND, DURING OUR INTERVIEW IN HIS LONDON RESIDENCE, BOTH REPELLENT AND FASCINATING...
...BUT WHOSE AQUILINE FACE HAUNTS MY DREAMS.
AND WHAT DO YOU DO HERE, THEN, AT THIS HOUSE, ON THIS NIGHT OF ALL NIGHTS?
FALCONMERE CASTLE LIES A GOOD TWENTY LEAGUES FROM HERE, ON THE OTHER SIDE OF THE MOORS.
THE COACHMAN--AN ILL-NATURED FELLOW, AND A MUTE, OR SO HE PRETENDED TO BE, FOR HE FORMED NO WORDS, BUT MADE HIS WISHES KNOWN ONLY BY GRUNTS AND GOBBLINGS--REINED IN HIS TEAM A MILE OR SO BACK DOWN THE ROAD, OR SO I JUDGE, AND THEN HE SHOWED ME BY GESTURES THAT HE WOULD GO NO FURTHER, AND THAT I WAS TO ALIGHT.
WHEN I DID REFUSE TO DO SO, HE PUSHED ME ROUGHLY FROM THE CARRIAGE TO THE COLD EARTH, THEN, WHIPPING THE POOR HORSES INTO A FRENZY, HE CLATTERED OFF THE WAY HE HAD COME, TAKING MY SEVERAL BAGS AND MY TRUNK WITH HIM.
I CALLED AFTER HIM, BUT HE DID NOT RETURN, AND IT SEEMED TO ME THAT A DEEPER DARKNESS STIRRED IN THE FOREST GLOOM BEHIND ME. I SAW THE LIGHT IN YOUR WINDOW AND I... I...
SOB!

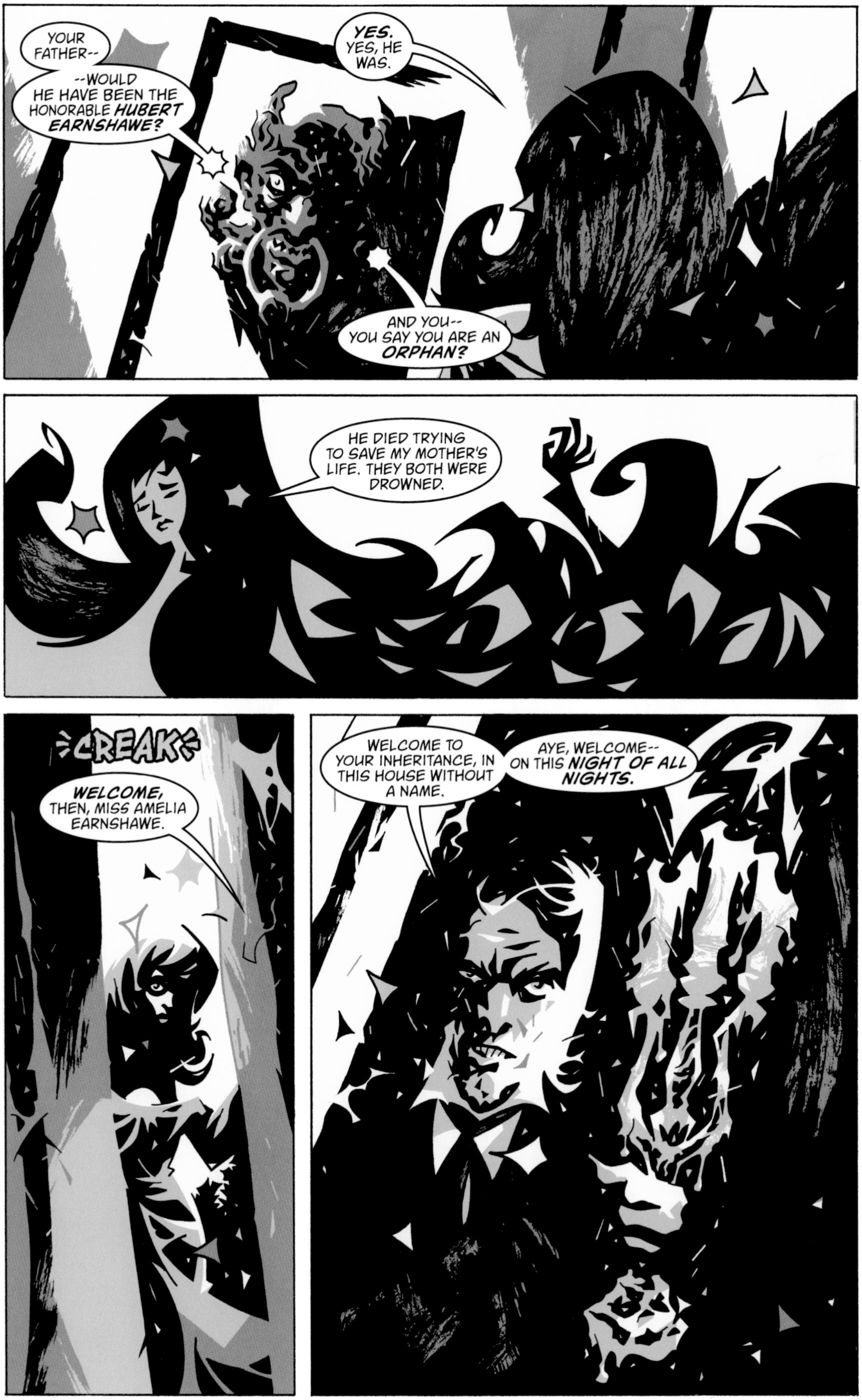
YOUR FATHER--
--WOULD HE HAVE BEEN THE HONORABLE HUBERT EARNSHAWE?
YES. YES, HE WAS.
AND YOU-- YOU SAY YOU ARE AN ORPHAN?
HE DIED TRYING TO SAVE MY MOTHER'S LIFE. THEY BOTH WERE DROWNED.
CREAK
WELCOME, THEN, MISS AMELIA EARNSHAWE.
WELCOME TO YOUR INHERITANCE, IN THIS HOUSE WITHOUT A NAME.
AYE, WELCOME-- ON THIS NIGHT OF ALL NIGHTS.

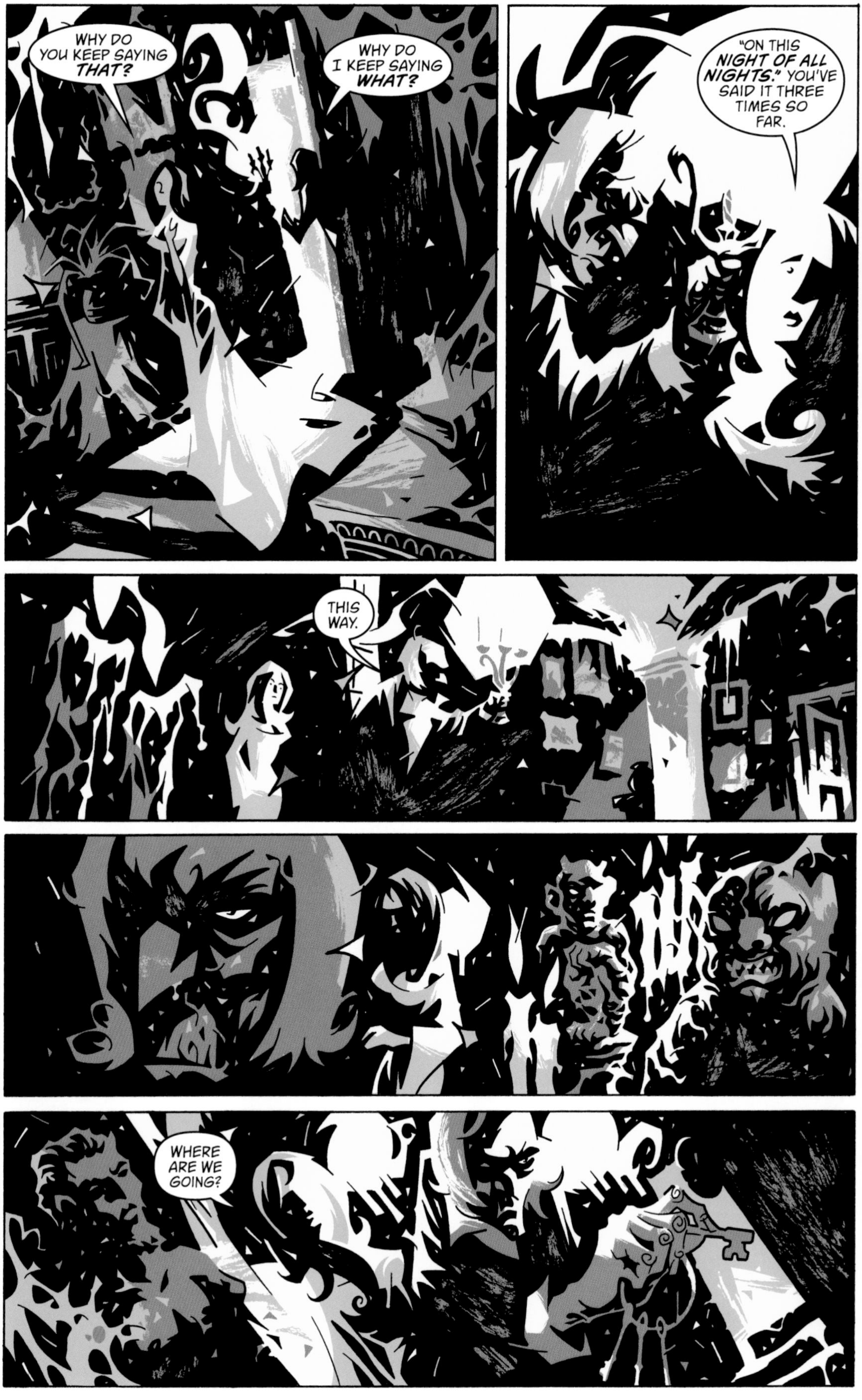

WHY DO YOU KEEP SAYING *THAT?*
WHY DO I KEEP SAYING *WHAT?*
"ON THIS *NIGHT OF ALL NIGHTS.*" YOU'VE SAID IT THREE TIMES SO FAR.
THIS WAY.
WHERE ARE WE GOING?

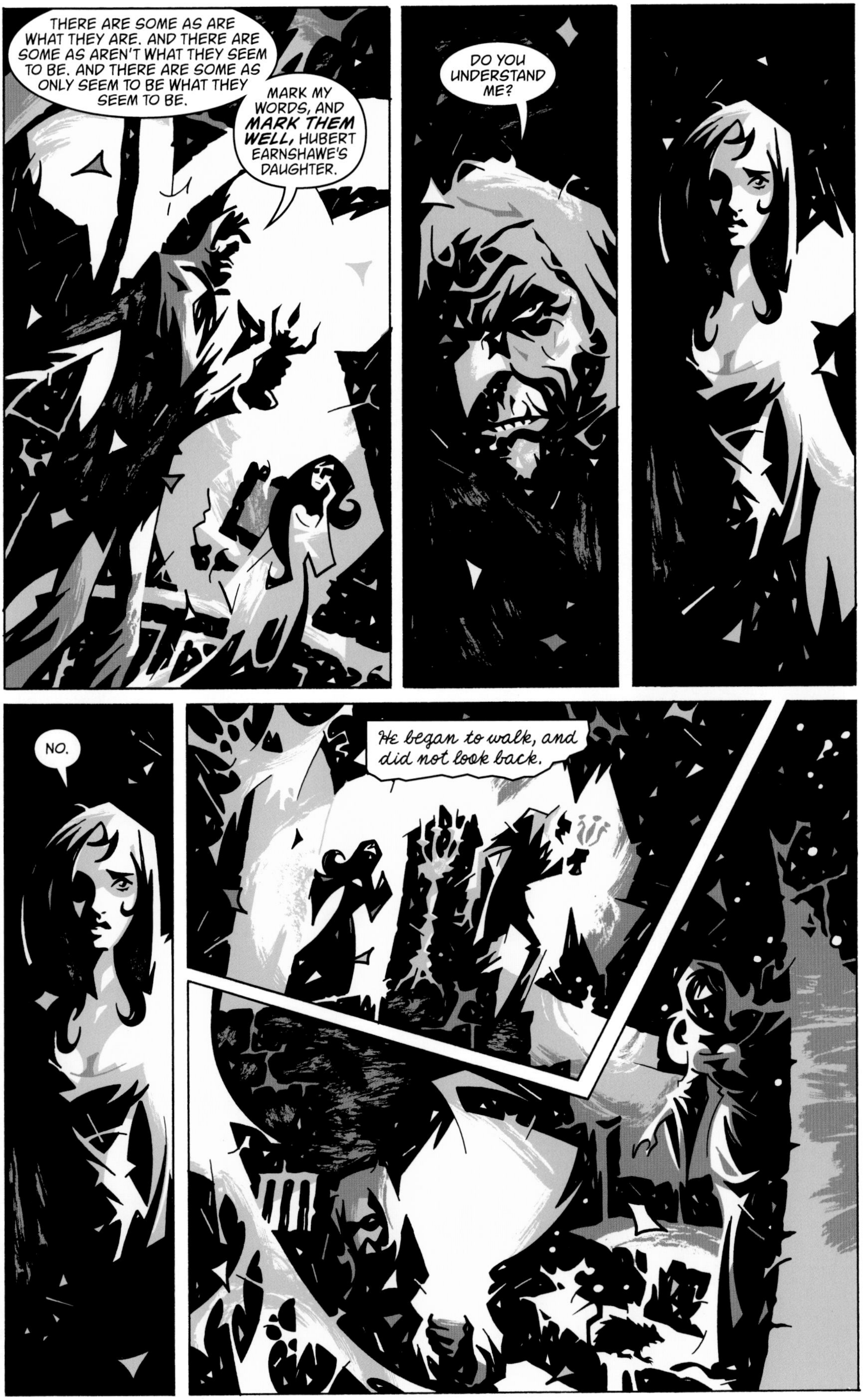
THERE ARE SOME AS ARE WHAT THEY ARE. AND THERE ARE SOME AS AREN'T WHAT THEY SEEM TO BE. AND THERE ARE SOME AS ONLY SEEM TO BE WHAT THEY SEEM TO BE.
MARK MY WORDS, AND **MARK THEM WELL,** HUBERT EARNSHAWE'S DAUGHTER.
DO YOU UNDERSTAND ME?
NO.
He began to walk, and did not look back.

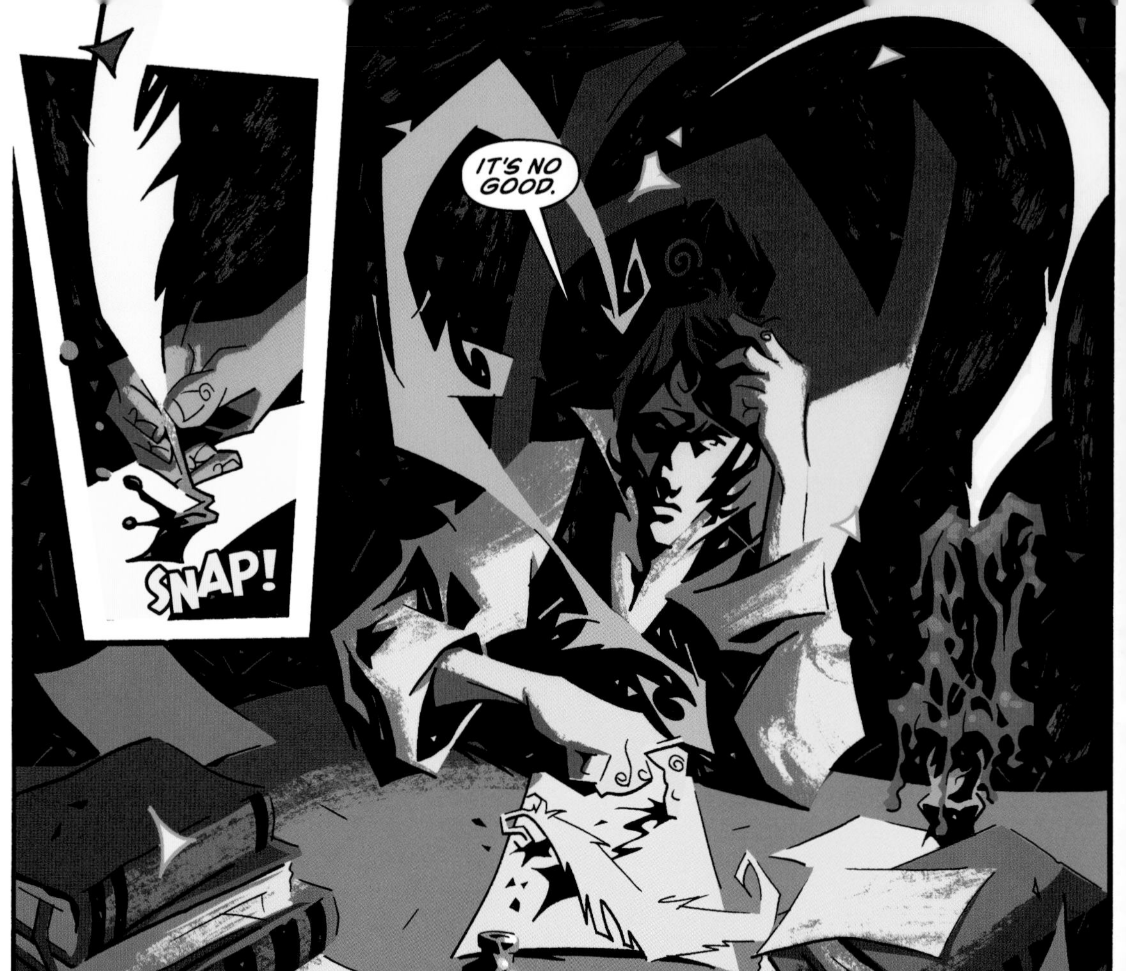
SNAP!
IT'S NO GOOD.

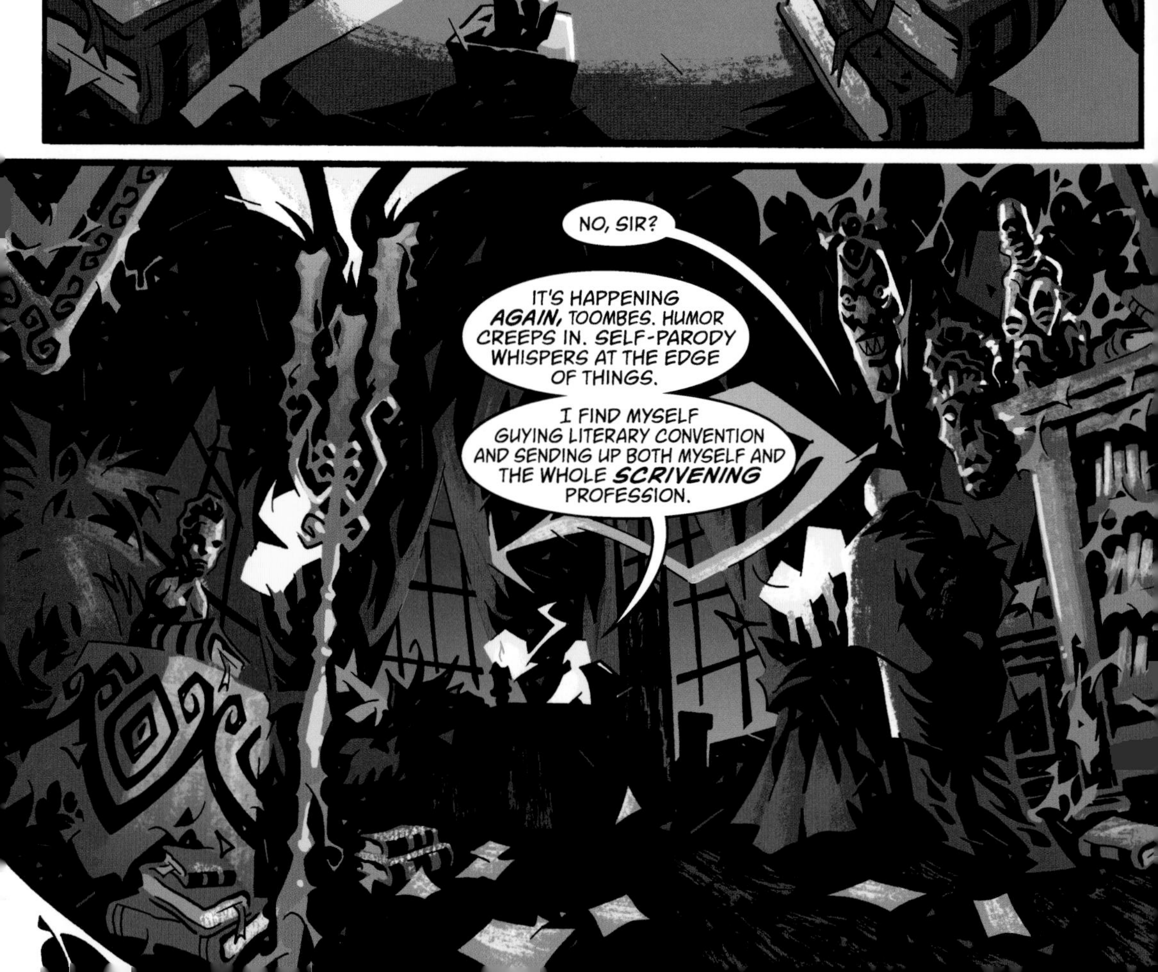
NO, SIR?
IT'S HAPPENING AGAIN, TOOMBES. HUMOR CREEPS IN. SELF-PARODY WHISPERS AT THE EDGE OF THINGS.
I FIND MYSELF GUYING LITERARY CONVENTION AND SENDING UP BOTH MYSELF AND THE WHOLE SCRIVENING PROFESSION.

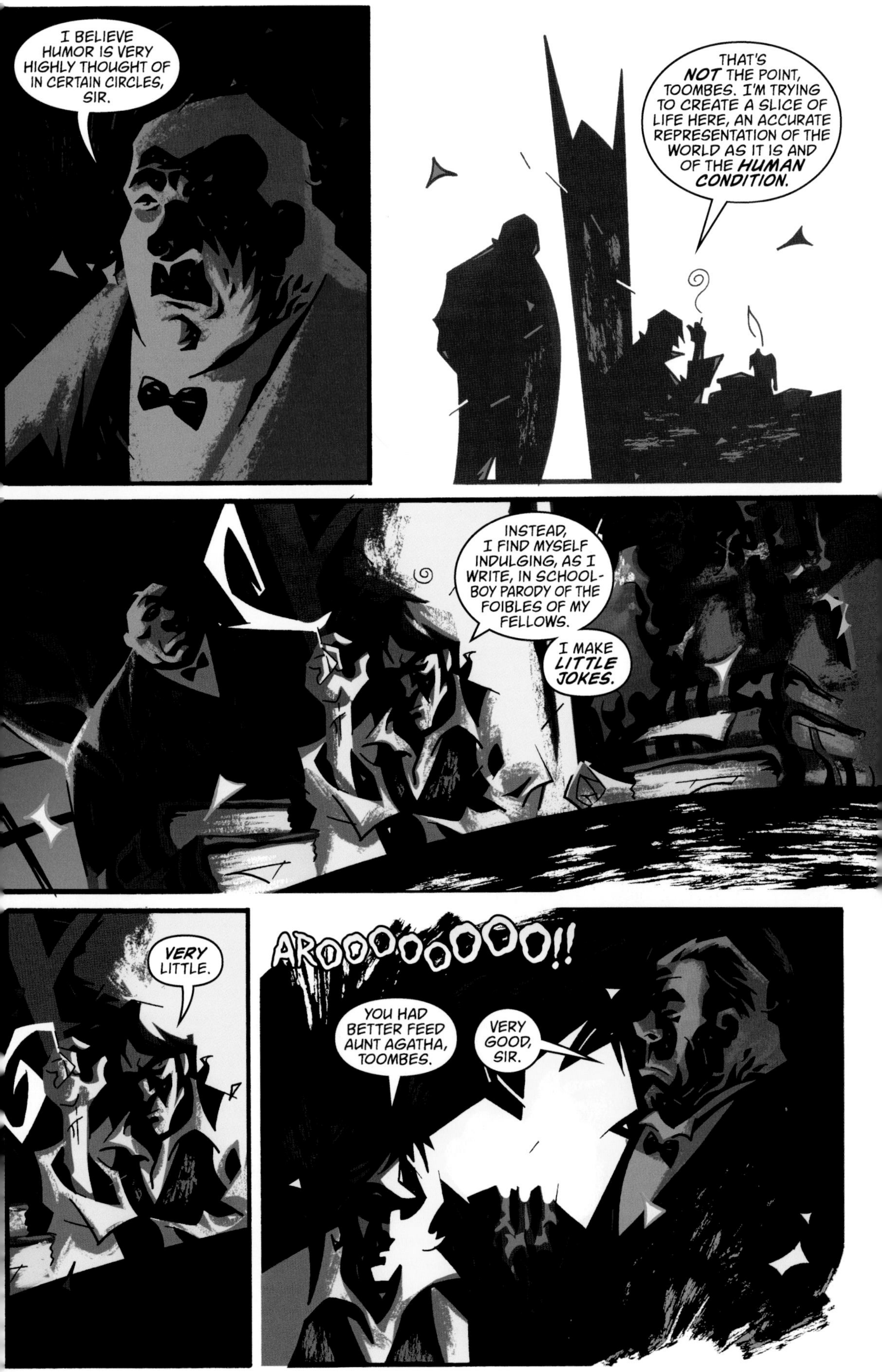
I BELIEVE HUMOR IS VERY HIGHLY THOUGHT OF IN CERTAIN CIRCLES, SIR.
THAT'S **NOT** THE POINT, TOOMBES. I'M TRYING TO CREATE A SLICE OF LIFE HERE, AN ACCURATE REPRESENTATION OF THE WORLD AS IT IS AND OF THE **HUMAN CONDITION.**
INSTEAD, I FIND MYSELF INDULGING, AS I WRITE, IN SCHOOL-BOY PARODY OF THE FOIBLES OF MY FELLOWS.
I MAKE **LITTLE JOKES.**
VERY LITTLE.
AROOOOOOOOO!!
YOU HAD BETTER FEED AUNT AGATHA, TOOMBES.
VERY GOOD, SIR.

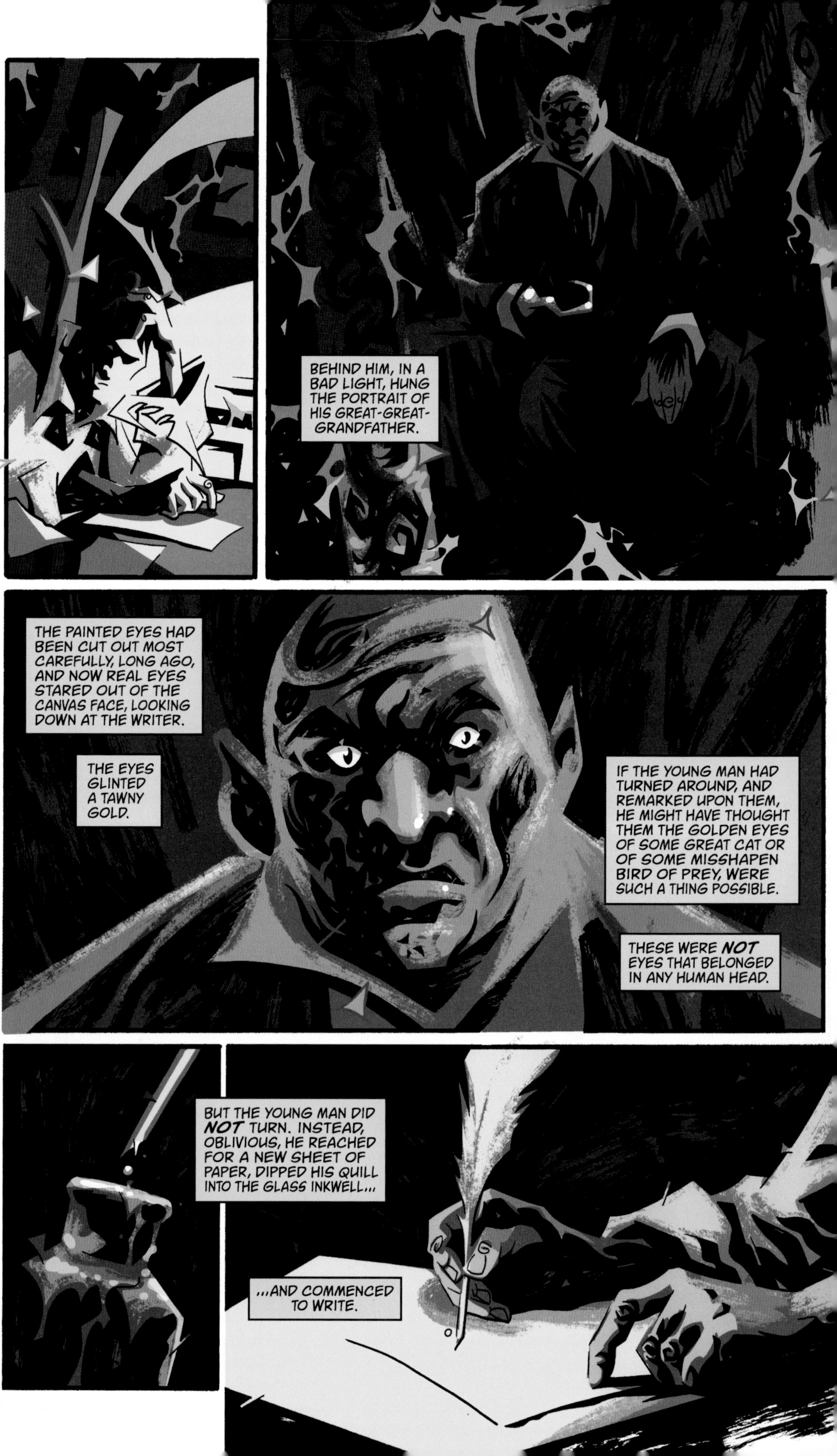
BEHIND HIM, IN A BAD LIGHT, HUNG THE PORTRAIT OF HIS GREAT-GREAT-GRANDFATHER.
THE PAINTED EYES HAD BEEN CUT OUT MOST CAREFULLY, LONG AGO, AND NOW REAL EYES STARED OUT OF THE CANVAS FACE, LOOKING DOWN AT THE WRITER.
THE EYES GLINTED A TAWNY GOLD.
IF THE YOUNG MAN HAD TURNED AROUND, AND REMARKED UPON THEM, HE MIGHT HAVE THOUGHT THEM THE GOLDEN EYES OF SOME GREAT CAT OR OF SOME MISSHAPEN BIRD OF PREY, WERE SUCH A THING POSSIBLE.
THESE WERE ***NOT*** EYES THAT BELONGED IN ANY HUMAN HEAD.
BUT THE YOUNG MAN DID ***NOT*** TURN. INSTEAD, OBLIVIOUS, HE REACHED FOR A NEW SHEET OF PAPER, DIPPED HIS QUILL INTO THE GLASS INKWELL...
...AND COMMENCED TO WRITE.

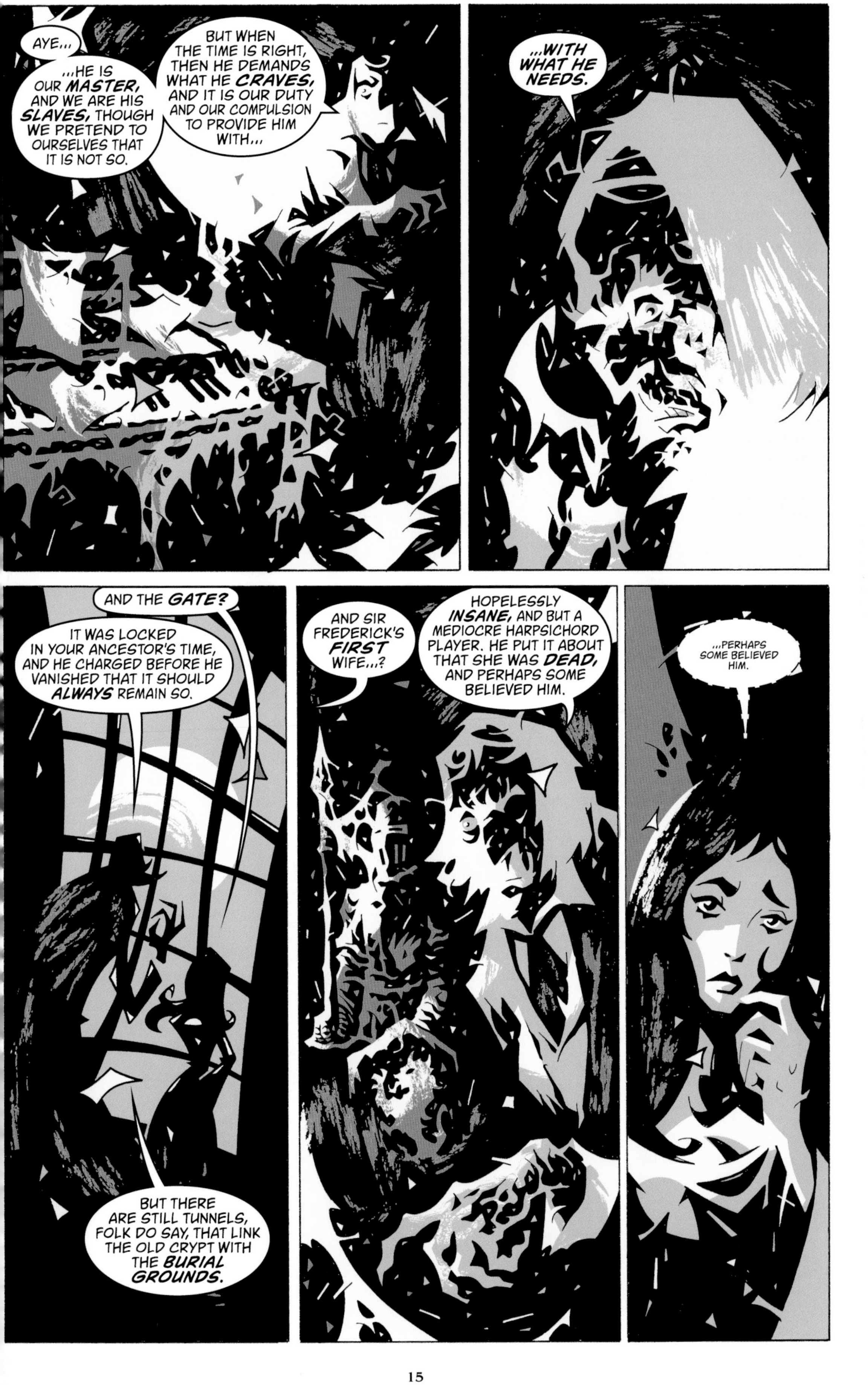
AYE...
...HE IS OUR MASTER, AND WE ARE HIS SLAVES, THOUGH WE PRETEND TO OURSELVES THAT IT IS NOT SO.
BUT WHEN THE TIME IS RIGHT, THEN HE DEMANDS WHAT HE CRAVES, AND IT IS OUR DUTY AND OUR COMPULSION TO PROVIDE HIM WITH...
...WITH WHAT HE NEEDS.
AND THE GATE?
IT WAS LOCKED IN YOUR ANCESTOR'S TIME, AND HE CHARGED BEFORE HE VANISHED THAT IT SHOULD ALWAYS REMAIN SO.
BUT THERE ARE STILL TUNNELS, FOLK DO SAY, THAT LINK THE OLD CRYPT WITH THE BURIAL GROUNDS.
AND SIR FREDERICK'S FIRST WIFE...?
HOPELESSLY INSANE, AND BUT A MEDIOCRE HARPSICHORD PLAYER. HE PUT IT ABOUT THAT SHE WAS DEAD, AND PERHAPS SOME BELIEVED HIM.
...PERHAPS SOME BELIEVED HIM.

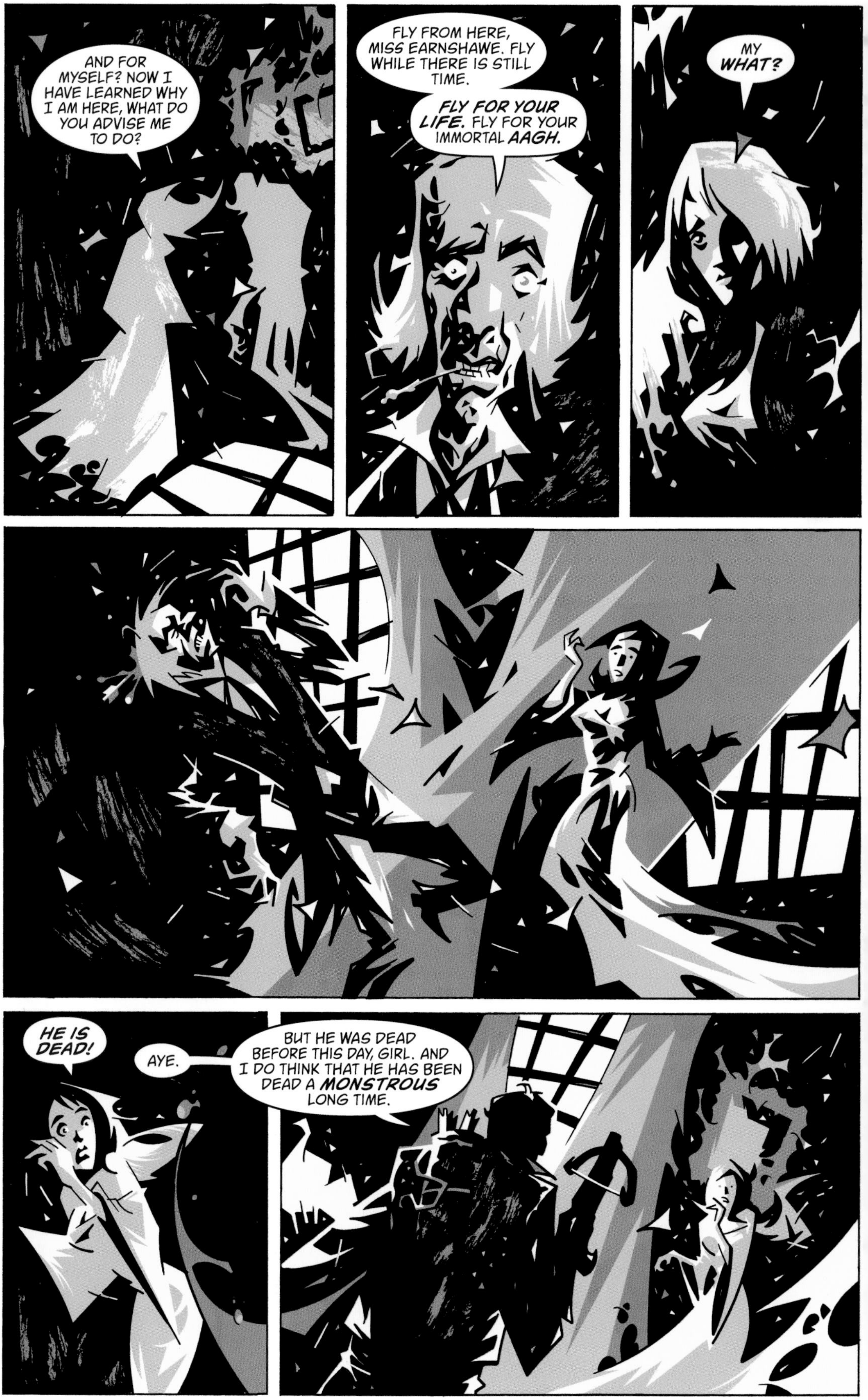
AND FOR MYSELF? NOW I HAVE LEARNED WHY I AM HERE, WHAT DO YOU ADVISE ME TO DO?
FLY FROM HERE, MISS EARNSHAWE. FLY WHILE THERE IS STILL TIME.
FLY FOR YOUR LIFE. FLY FOR YOUR IMMORTAL AAGH.
MY WHAT?
HE IS DEAD!
AYE.
BUT HE WAS DEAD BEFORE THIS DAY, GIRL. AND I DO THINK THAT HE HAS BEEN DEAD A MONSTROUS LONG TIME.

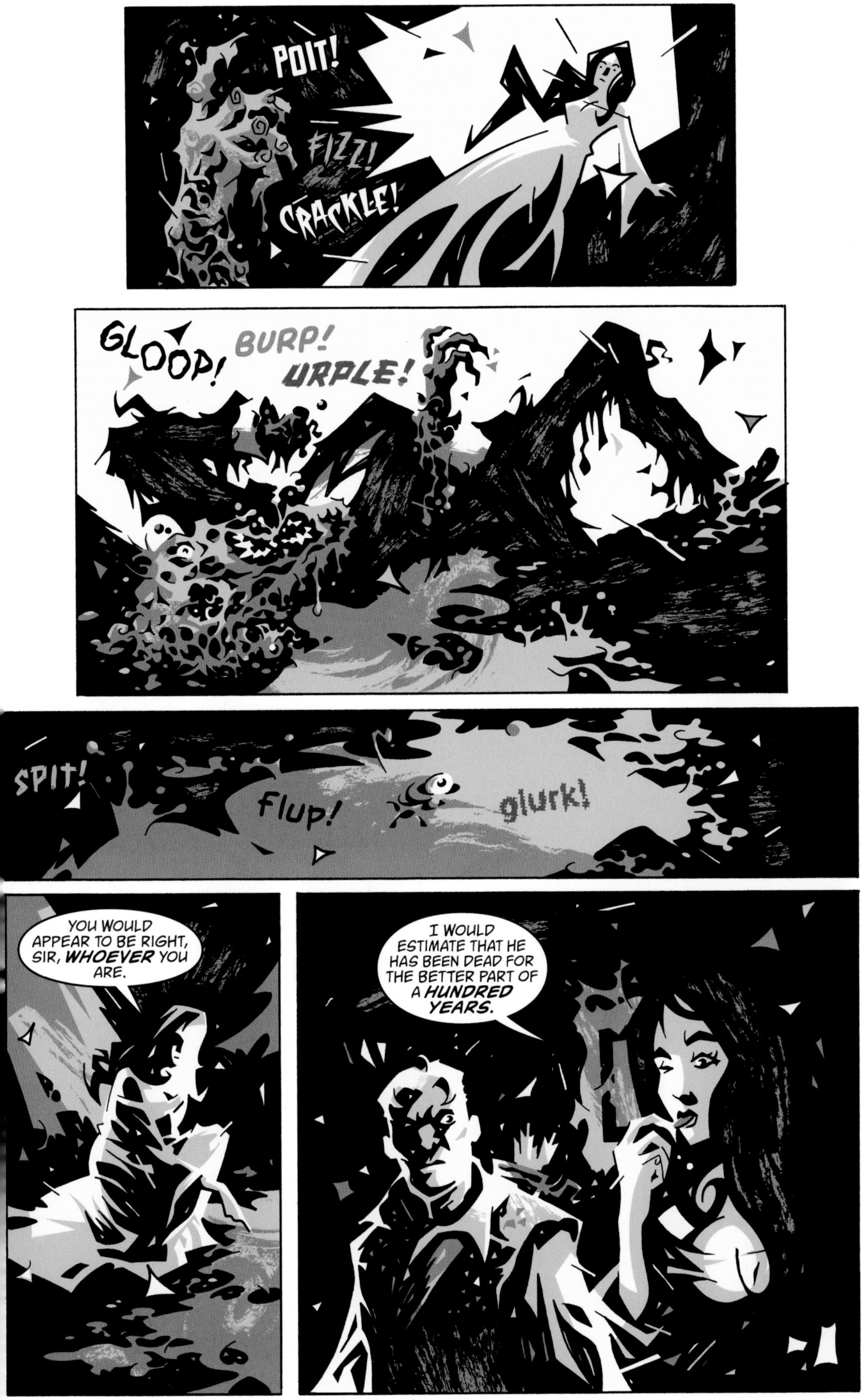
POIT!
FIZZ!
CRACKLE!
GLOOP!
BURP!
URPLE!
SPIT!
flup!
glurk!
YOU WOULD APPEAR TO BE RIGHT, SIR, ***WHOEVER*** YOU ARE.
I WOULD ESTIMATE THAT HE HAS BEEN DEAD FOR THE BETTER PART OF A ***HUNDRED YEARS.***

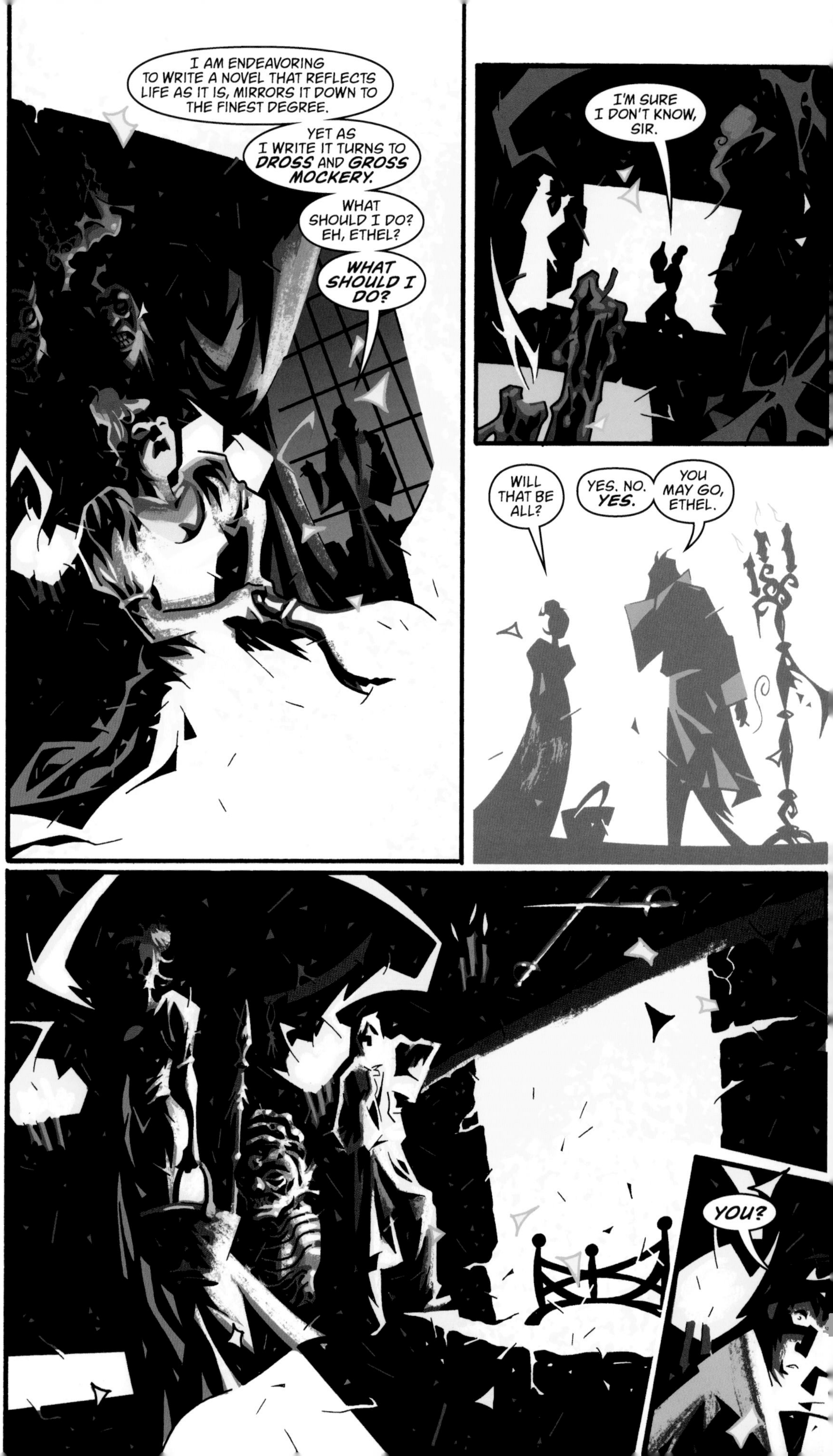

I AM ENDEAVORING TO WRITE A NOVEL THAT REFLECTS LIFE AS IT IS, MIRRORS IT DOWN TO THE FINEST DEGREE.
YET AS I WRITE IT TURNS TO DROSS AND GROSS MOCKERY.
WHAT SHOULD I DO? EH, ETHEL?
WHAT SHOULD I DO?
I'M SURE I DON'T KNOW, SIR.
WILL THAT BE ALL?
YES. NO. YES.
YOU MAY GO, ETHEL.
YOU?

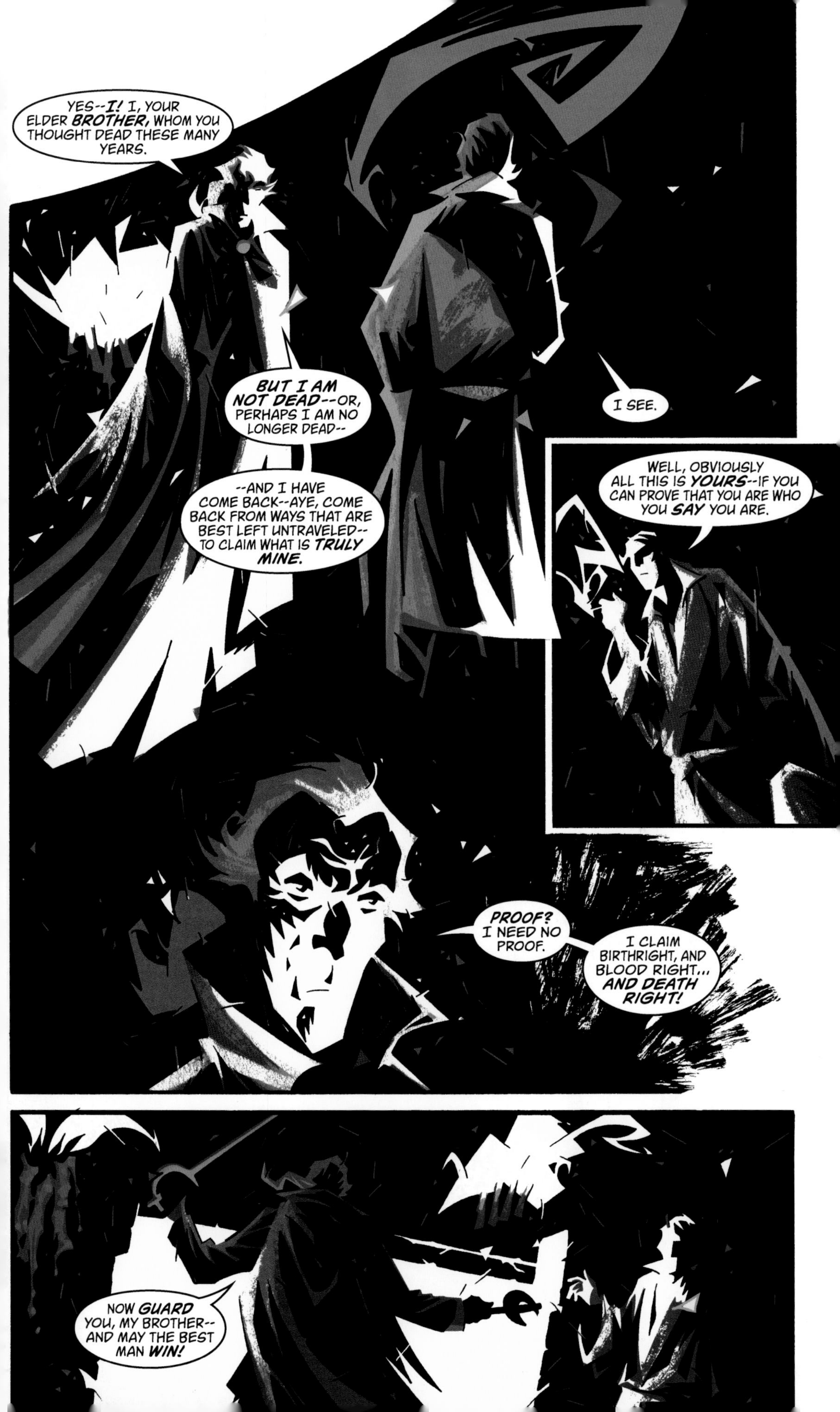
YES--I! I, YOUR ELDER BROTHER, WHOM YOU THOUGHT DEAD THESE MANY YEARS.
BUT I AM NOT DEAD--OR, PERHAPS I AM NO LONGER DEAD--
--AND I HAVE COME BACK--AYE, COME BACK FROM WAYS THAT ARE BEST LEFT UNTRAVELED--TO CLAIM WHAT IS TRULY MINE.
I SEE.
WELL, OBVIOUSLY ALL THIS IS YOURS--IF YOU CAN PROVE THAT YOU ARE WHO YOU SAY YOU ARE.
PROOF? I NEED NO PROOF.
I CLAIM BIRTHRIGHT, AND BLOOD RIGHT... AND DEATH RIGHT!
NOW GUARD YOU, MY BROTHER--AND MAY THE BEST MAN WIN!

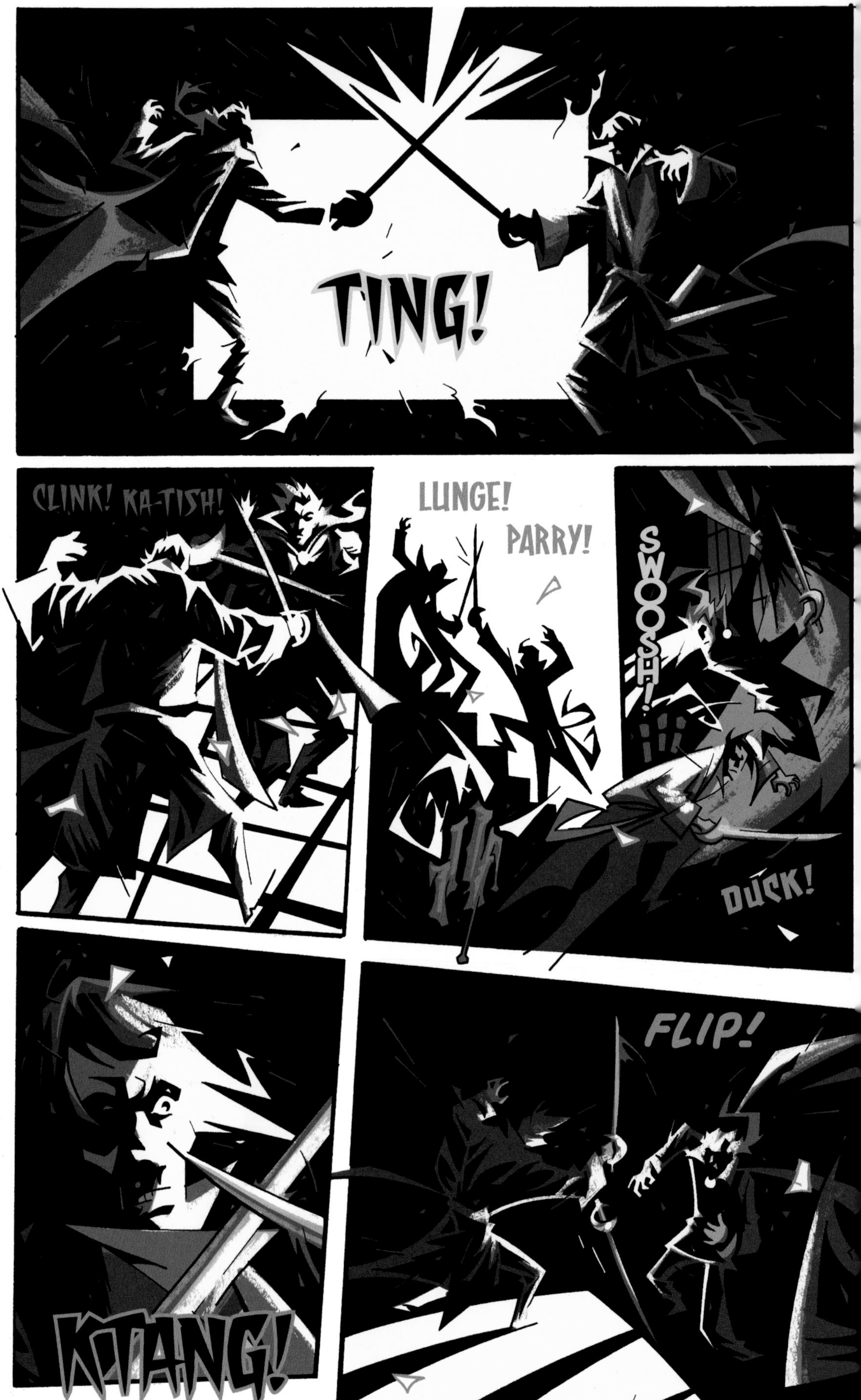
TING!
CLINK! KA-TISH!
LUNGE!
PARRY!
SWOOSH!
DUCK!
KTANG!
FLIP!

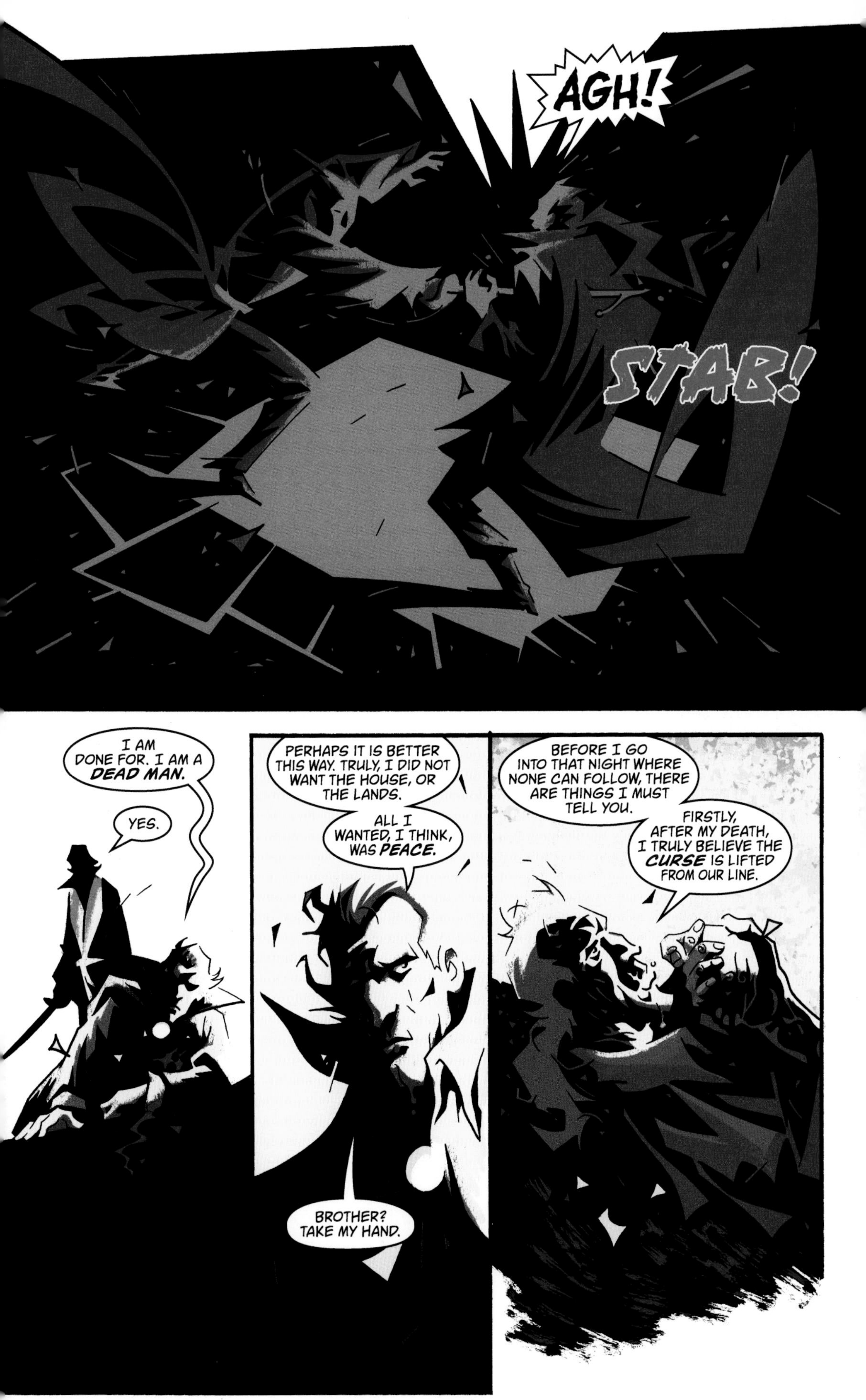
AGH!
STAB!
I AM DONE FOR. I AM A DEAD MAN.
YES.
PERHAPS IT IS BETTER THIS WAY. TRULY, I DID NOT WANT THE HOUSE, OR THE LANDS.
ALL I WANTED, I THINK, WAS PEACE.
BROTHER? TAKE MY HAND.
BEFORE I GO INTO THAT NIGHT WHERE NONE CAN FOLLOW, THERE ARE THINGS I MUST TELL YOU.
FIRSTLY, AFTER MY DEATH, I TRULY BELIEVE THE CURSE IS LIFTED FROM OUR LINE.

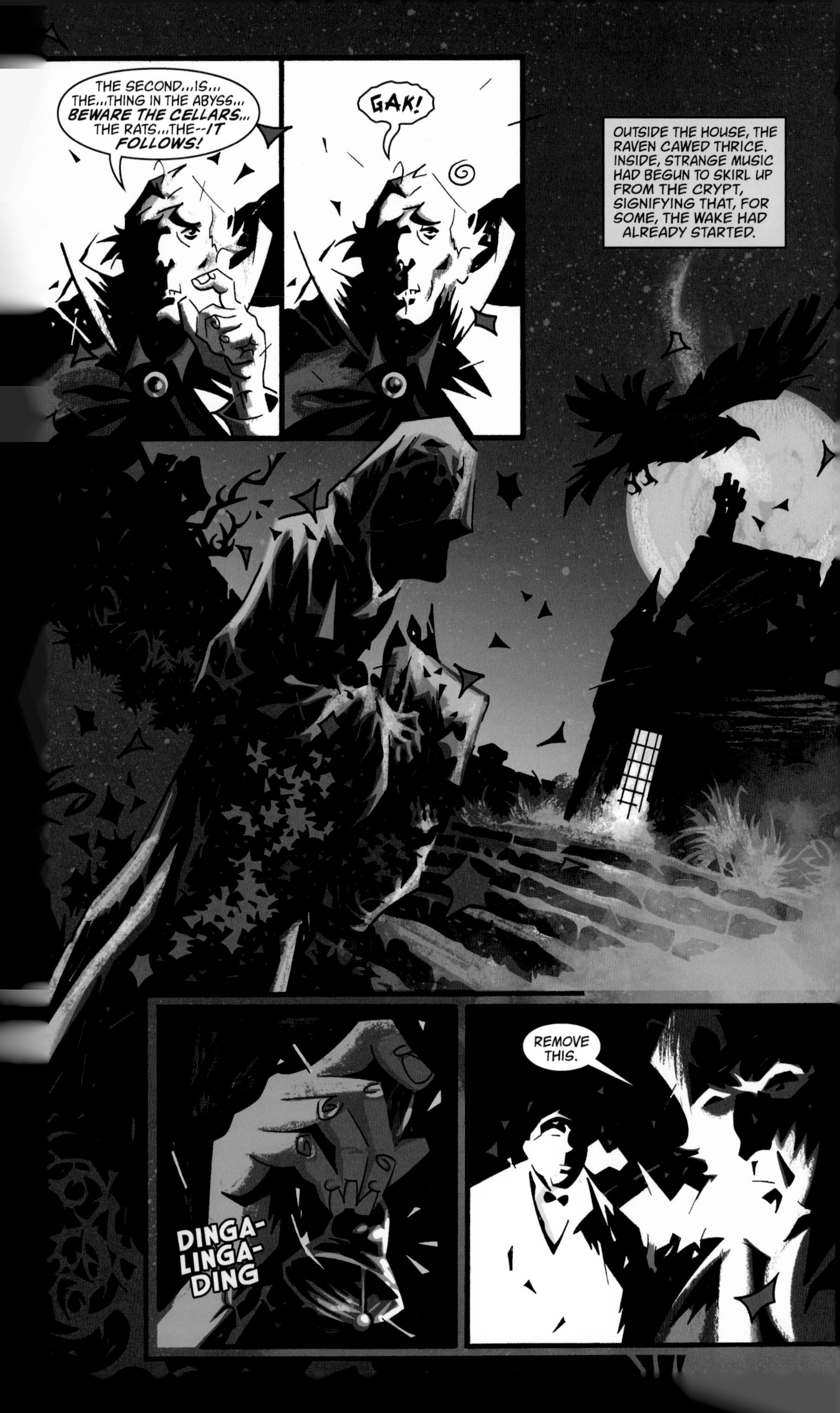
THE SECOND...IS... THE...THING IN THE ABYSS... *BEWARE THE CELLARS*... THE RATS...THE--*IT FOLLOWS!*
GAK!
OUTSIDE THE HOUSE, THE RAVEN CAWED THRICE. INSIDE, STRANGE MUSIC HAD BEGUN TO SKIRL UP FROM THE CRYPT, SIGNIFYING THAT, FOR SOME, THE WAKE HAD ALREADY STARTED.
DINGA-LINGA-DING
REMOVE THIS.

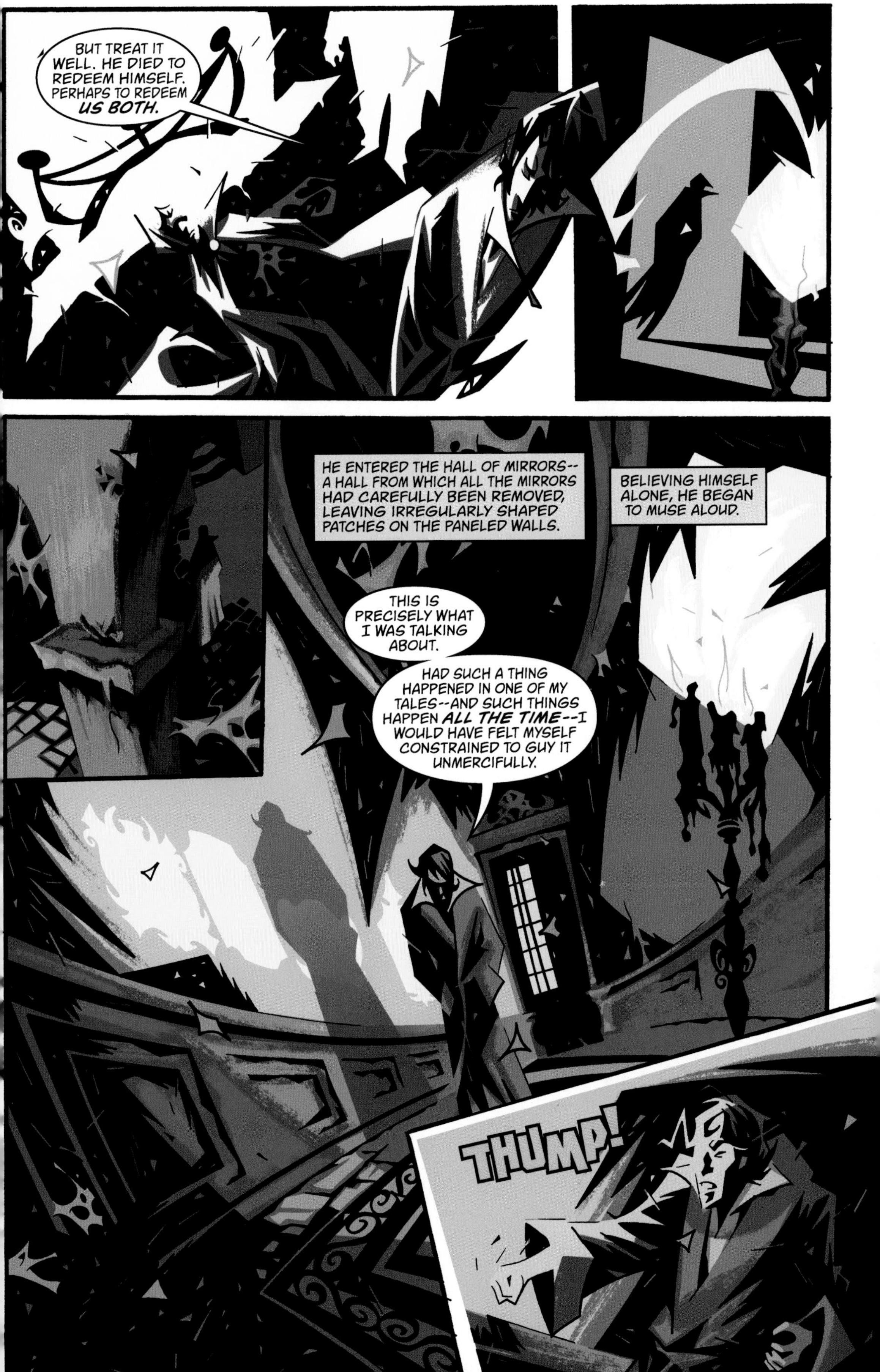

BUT TREAT IT WELL. HE DIED TO REDEEM HIMSELF. PERHAPS TO REDEEM US BOTH.
HE ENTERED THE HALL OF MIRRORS-- A HALL FROM WHICH ALL THE MIRRORS HAD CAREFULLY BEEN REMOVED, LEAVING IRREGULARLY SHAPED PATCHES ON THE PANELED WALLS.
BELIEVING HIMSELF ALONE, HE BEGAN TO MUSE ALOUD.
THIS IS PRECISELY WHAT I WAS TALKING ABOUT.
HAD SUCH A THING HAPPENED IN ONE OF MY TALES--AND SUCH THINGS HAPPEN ALL THE TIME--I WOULD HAVE FELT MYSELF CONSTRAINED TO GUY IT UNMERCIFULLY.
THUMP!

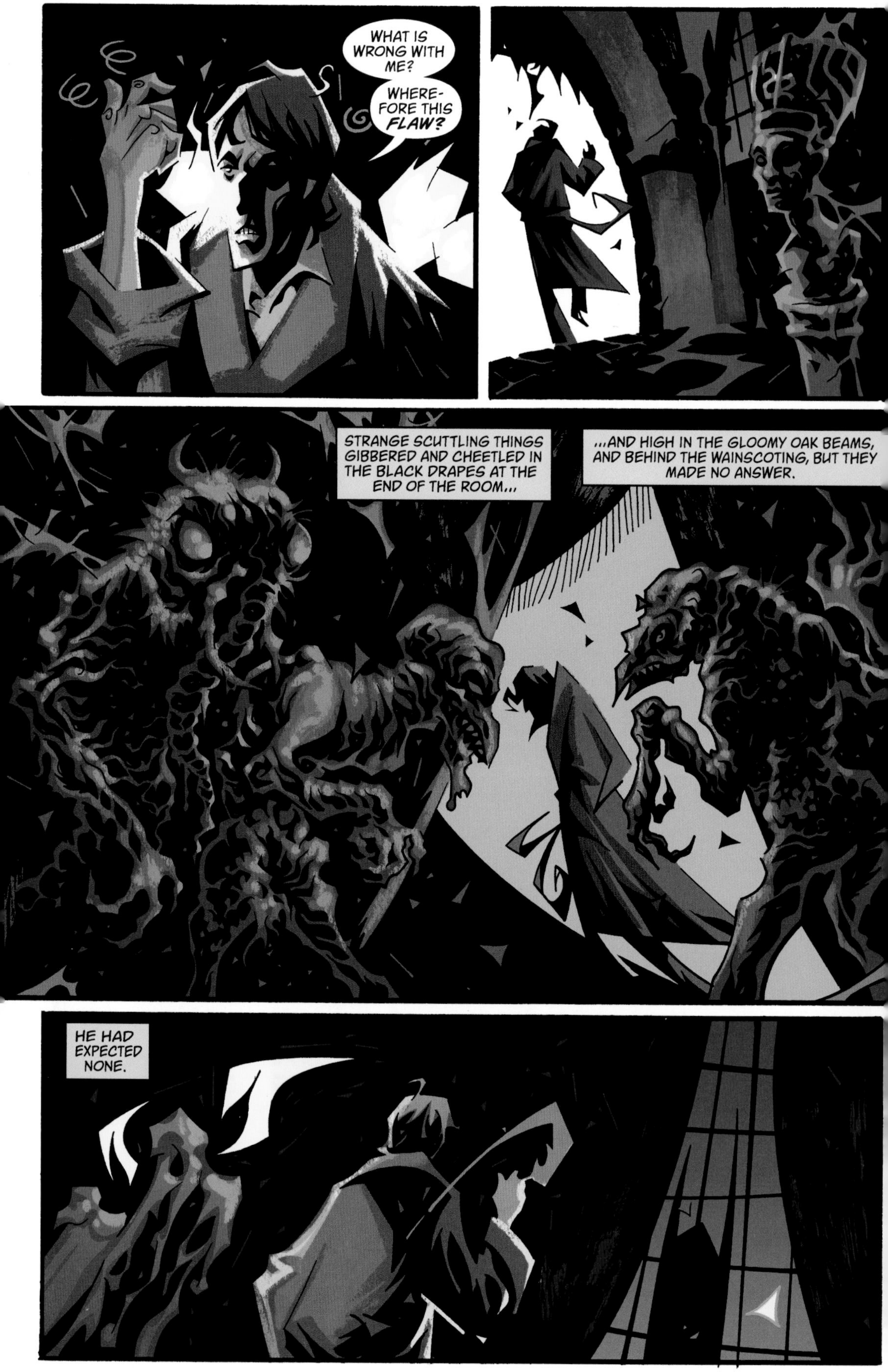
WHAT IS WRONG WITH ME?
WHERE-FORE THIS *FLAW?*
STRANGE SCUTTLING THINGS GIBBERED AND CHEETLED IN THE BLACK DRAPES AT THE END OF THE ROOM...
...AND HIGH IN THE GLOOMY OAK BEAMS, AND BEHIND THE WAINSCOTING, BUT THEY MADE NO ANSWER.
HE HAD EXPECTED NONE.

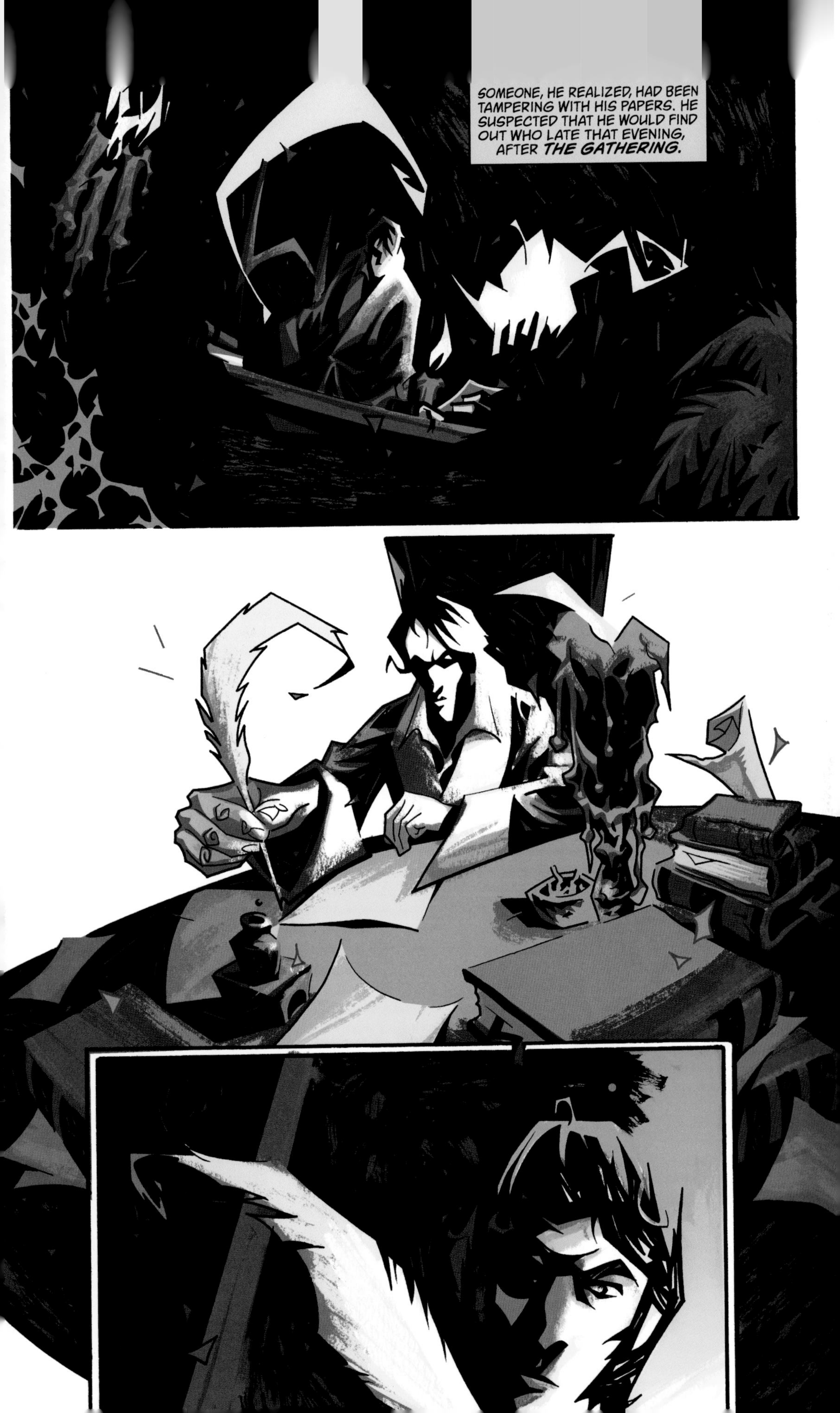
SOMEONE, HE REALIZED, HAD BEEN TAMPERING WITH HIS PAPERS. HE SUSPECTED THAT HE WOULD FIND OUT WHO LATE THAT EVENING, AFTER THE GATHERING.

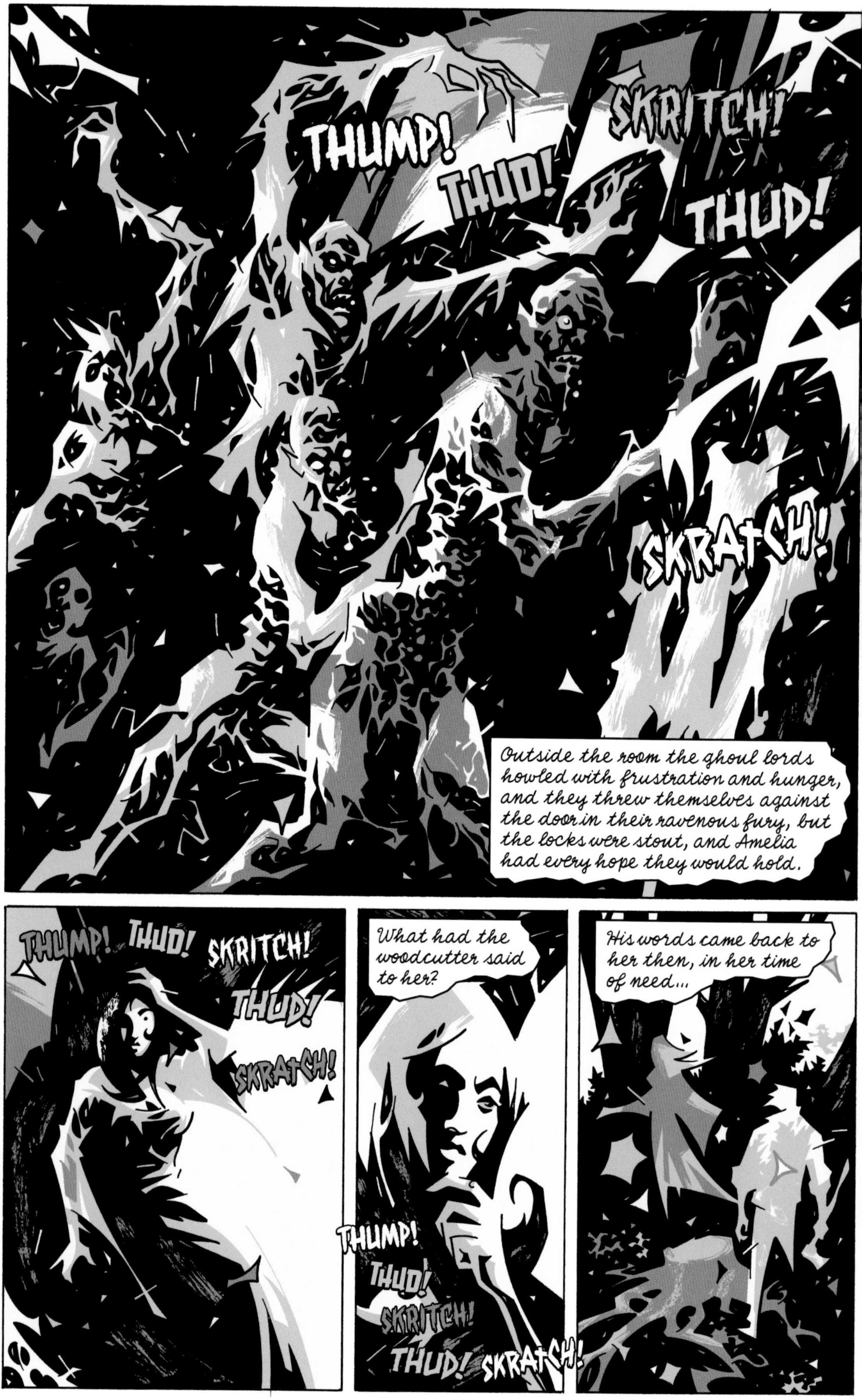
THUMP!
THUD!
SKRITCH!
THUD!
SKRATCH!
Outside the room the ghoul lords howled with frustration and hunger, and they threw themselves against the door in their ravenous fury, but the locks were stout, and Amelia had every hope they would hold.
THUMP! THUD! SKRITCH!
THUD!
SKRATCH!
What had the woodcutter said to her?
THUMP!
THUD!
SKRITCH!
THUD! SKRATCH!
His words came back to her then, in her time of need...

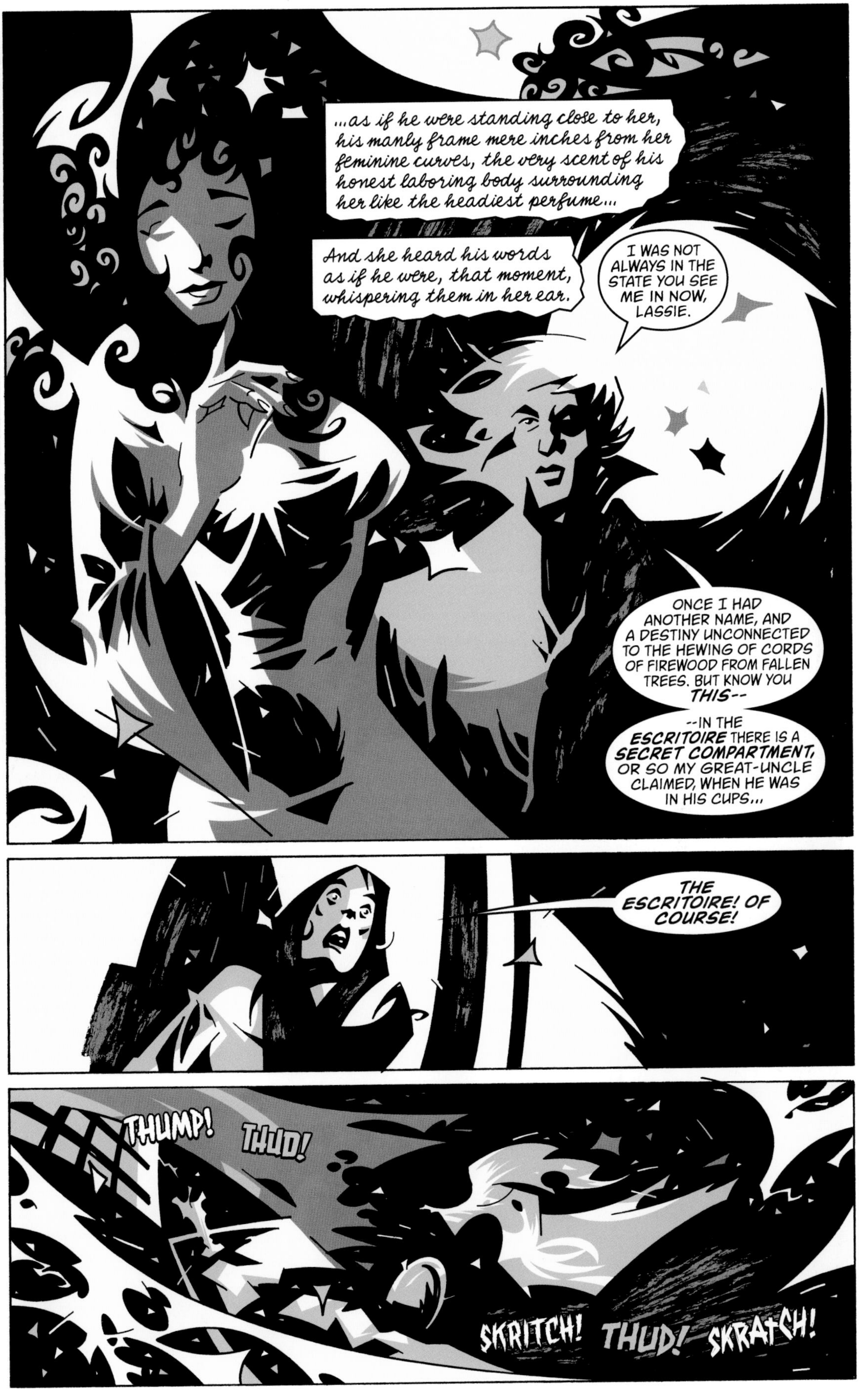
...as if he were standing close to her, his manly frame mere inches from her feminine curves, the very scent of his honest laboring body surrounding her like the headiest perfume...
And she heard his words as if he were, that moment, whispering them in her ear.
I WAS NOT ALWAYS IN THE STATE YOU SEE ME IN NOW, LASSIE.
ONCE I HAD ANOTHER NAME, AND A DESTINY UNCONNECTED TO THE HEWING OF CORDS OF FIREWOOD FROM FALLEN TREES. BUT KNOW YOU *THIS*--
--IN THE *ESCRITOIRE* THERE IS A *SECRET COMPARTMENT*, OR SO MY GREAT-UNCLE CLAIMED, WHEN HE WAS IN HIS CUPS...
THE ESCRITOIRE! OF COURSE!
THUMP! THUD!
SKRITCH! THUD! SKRATCH!

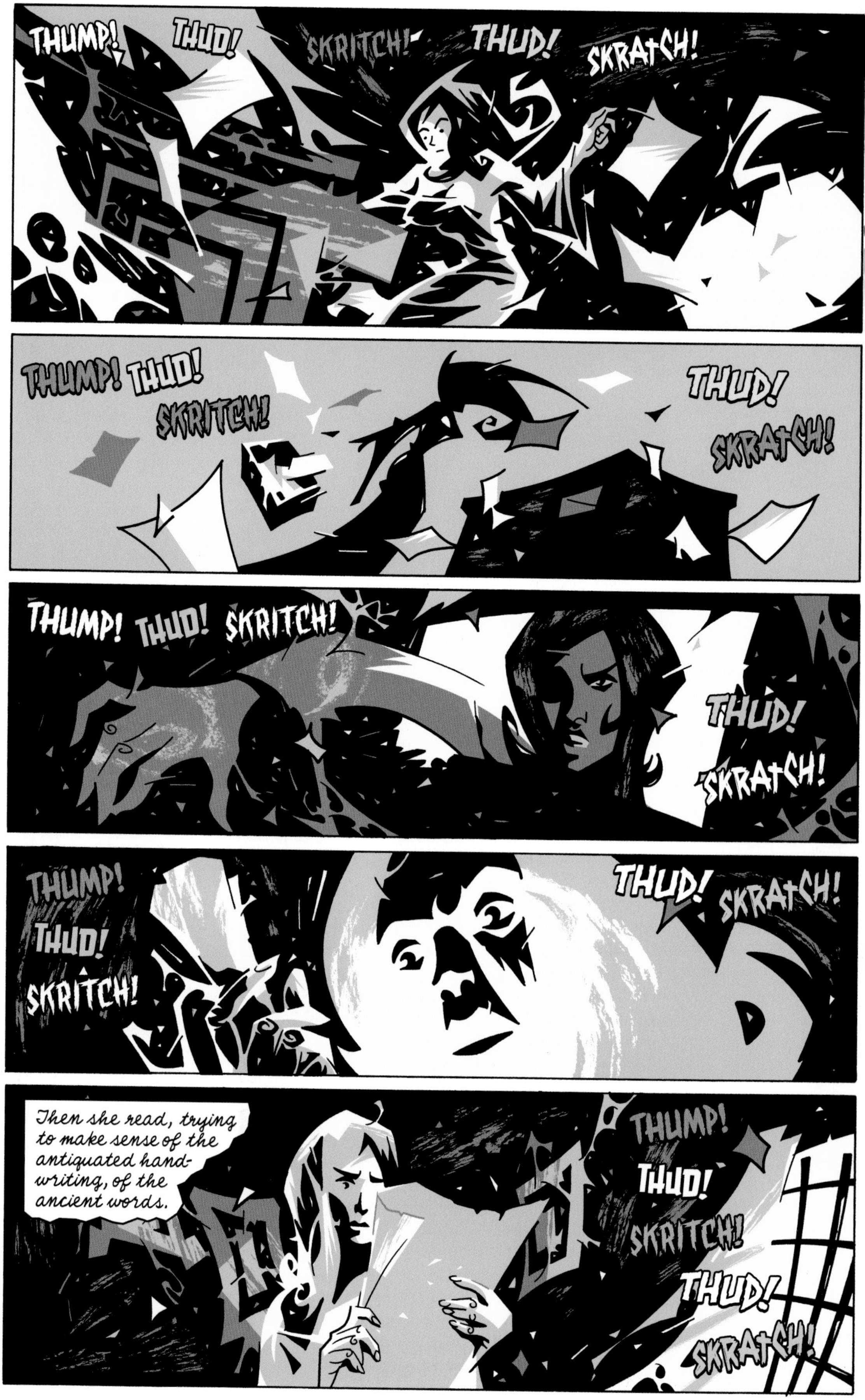
THUMP!
THUD!
SKRITCH!
THUD!
SKRATCH!
THUMP!
THUD!
SKRITCH!
THUD!
SKRATCH!
THUMP!
THUD!
SKRITCH!
THUD!
SKRATCH!
THUMP!
THUD!
SKRITCH!
THUD!
SKRATCH!
Then she read, trying to make sense of the antiquated handwriting, of the ancient words.
THUMP!
THUD!
SKRITCH!
THUD!
SKRATCH!

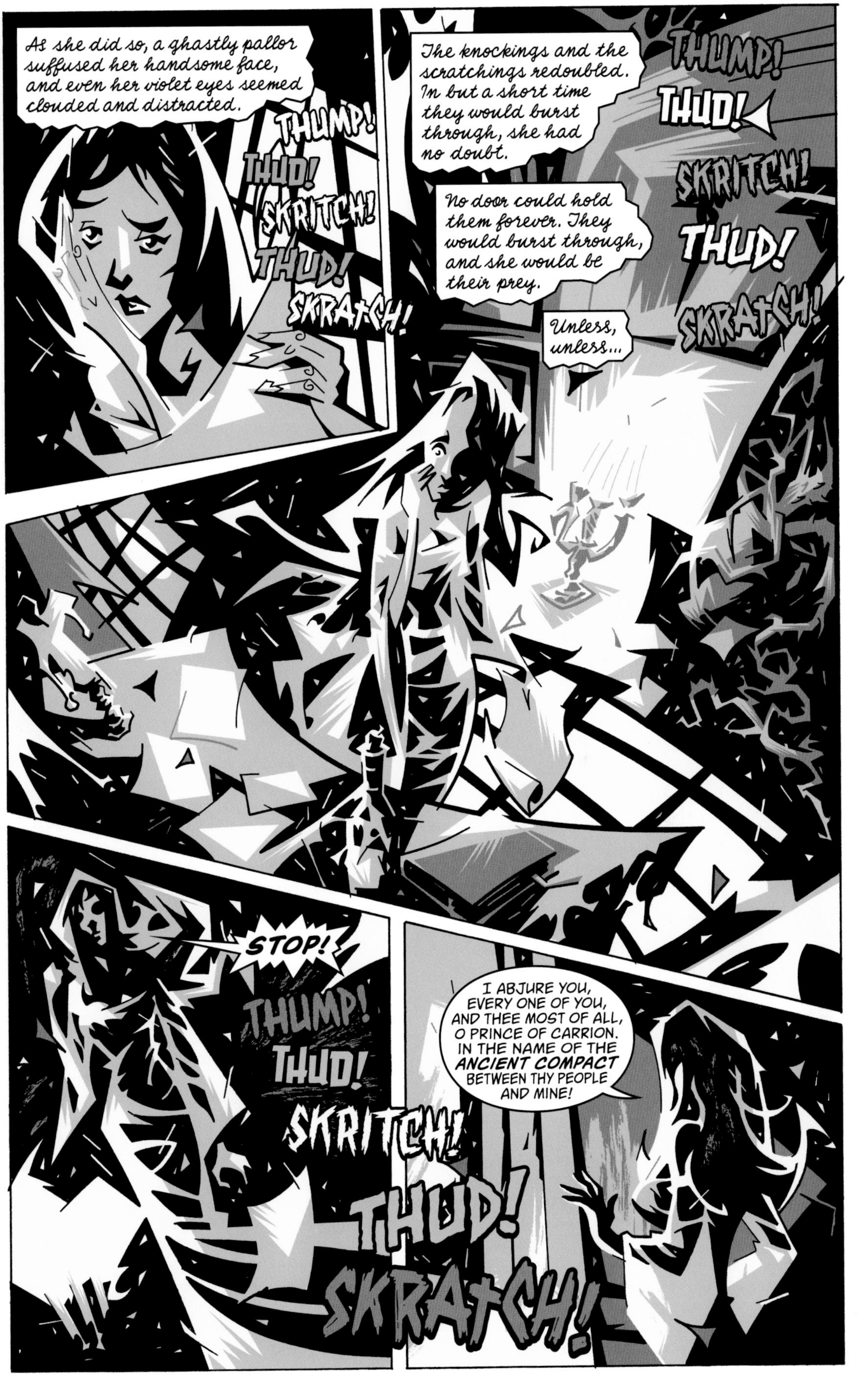
As she did so, a ghastly pallor suffused her handsome face, and even her violet eyes seemed clouded and distracted.
THUMP!
THUD!
SKRITCH!
THUD!
SKRATCH!
The knockings and the scratchings redoubled. In but a short time they would burst through, she had no doubt.
THUMP!
THUD!
SKRITCH!
THUD!
SKRATCH!
No door could hold them forever. They would burst through, and she would be their prey.
Unless, unless...
STOP!
THUMP!
THUD!
SKRITCH!
THUD!
SKRATCH!
I ABJURE YOU, EVERY ONE OF YOU, AND THEE MOST OF ALL, O PRINCE OF CARRION. IN THE NAME OF THE ***ANCIENT COMPACT*** BETWEEN THY PEOPLE AND MINE!

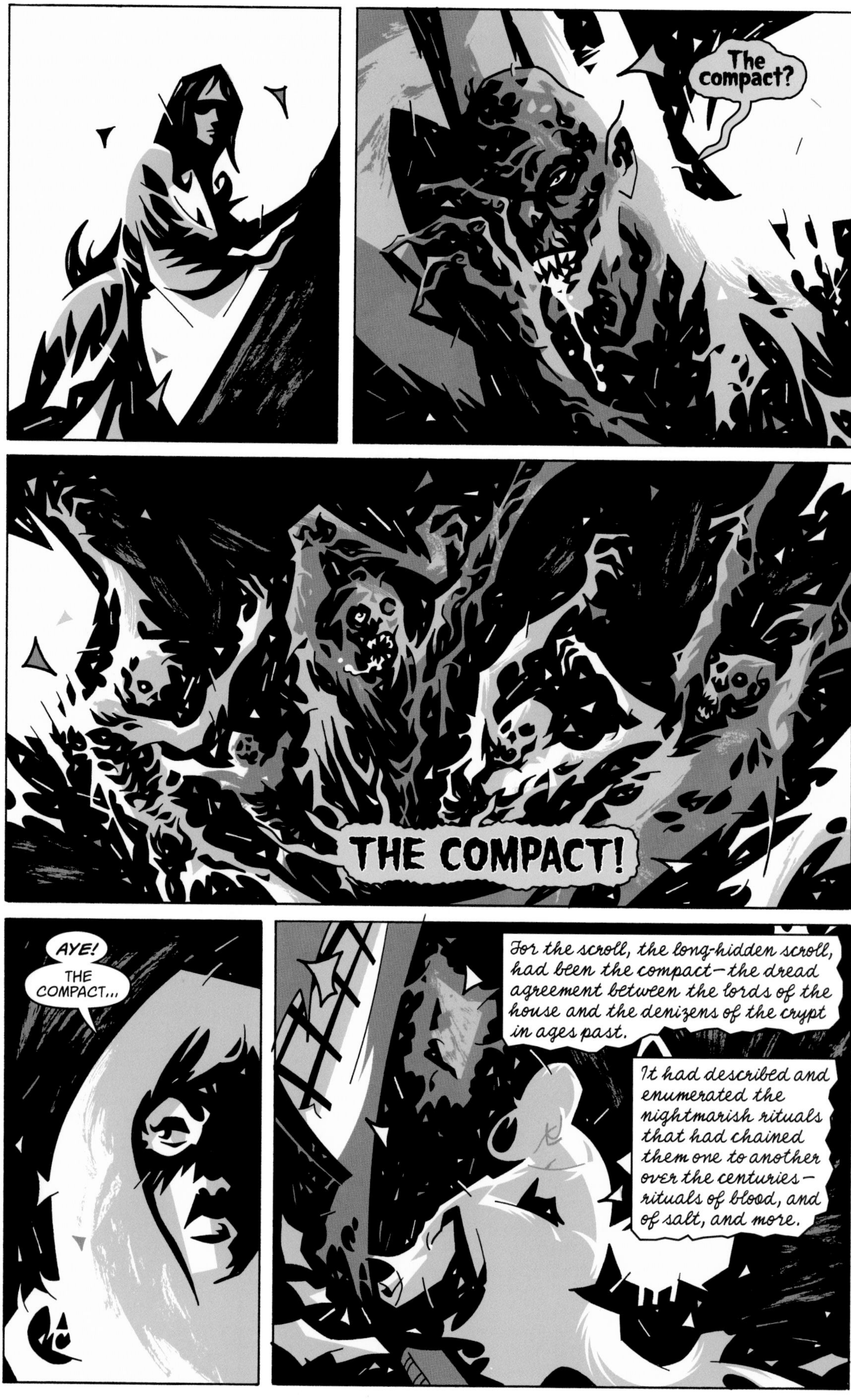
The compact?
THE COMPACT!
AYE! THE COMPACT...
For the scroll, the long-hidden scroll, had been the compact—the dread agreement between the lords of the house and the denizens of the crypt in ages past.
It had described and enumerated the nightmarish rituals that had chained them one to another over the centuries—rituals of blood, and of salt, and more.

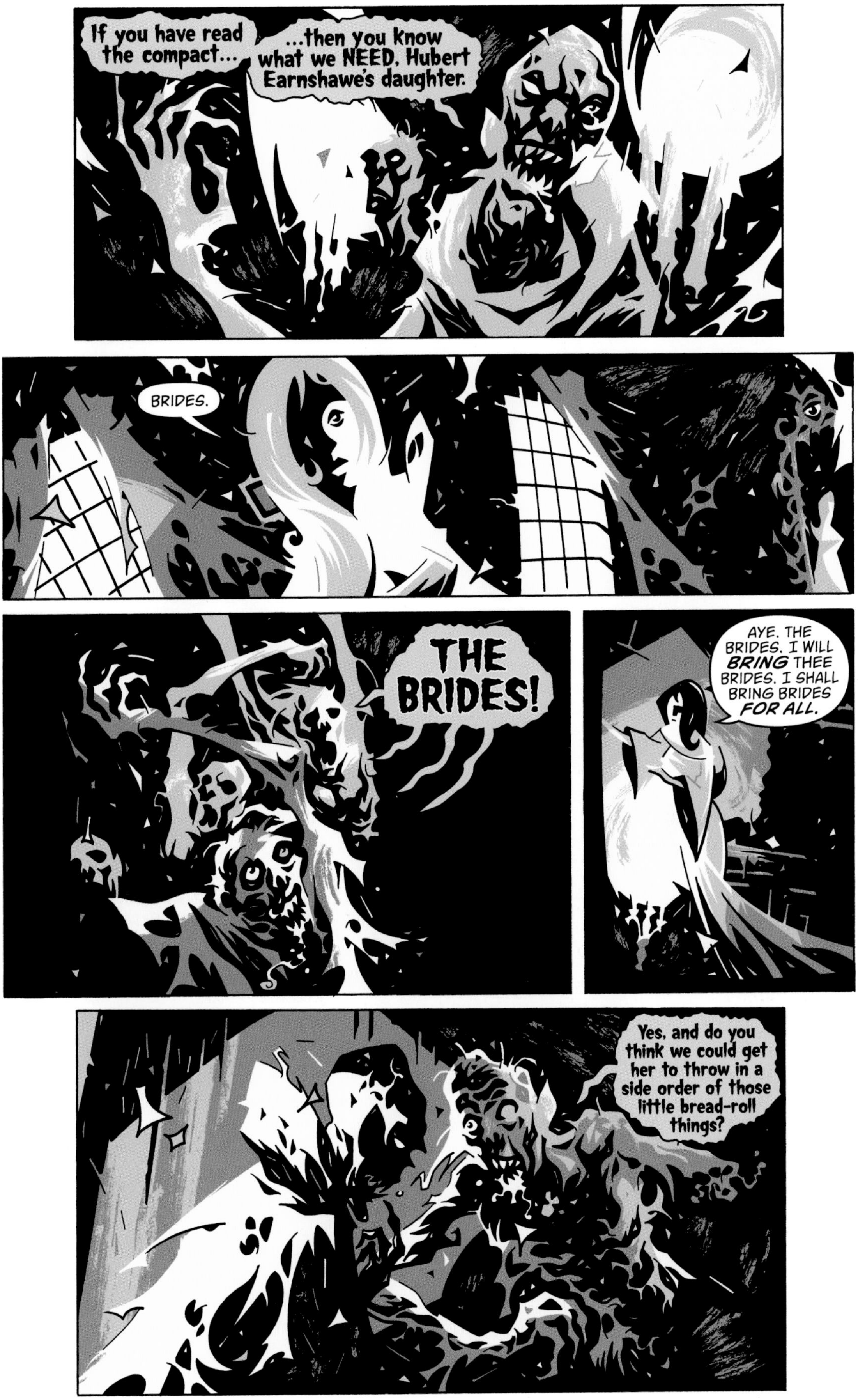
If you have read the compact...
...then you know what we NEED, Hubert Earnshawe's daughter.
BRIDES.
THE BRIDES!
AYE. THE BRIDES. I WILL BRING THEE BRIDES. I SHALL BRING BRIDES FOR ALL.
Yes, and do you think we could get her to throw in a side order of those little bread-roll things?

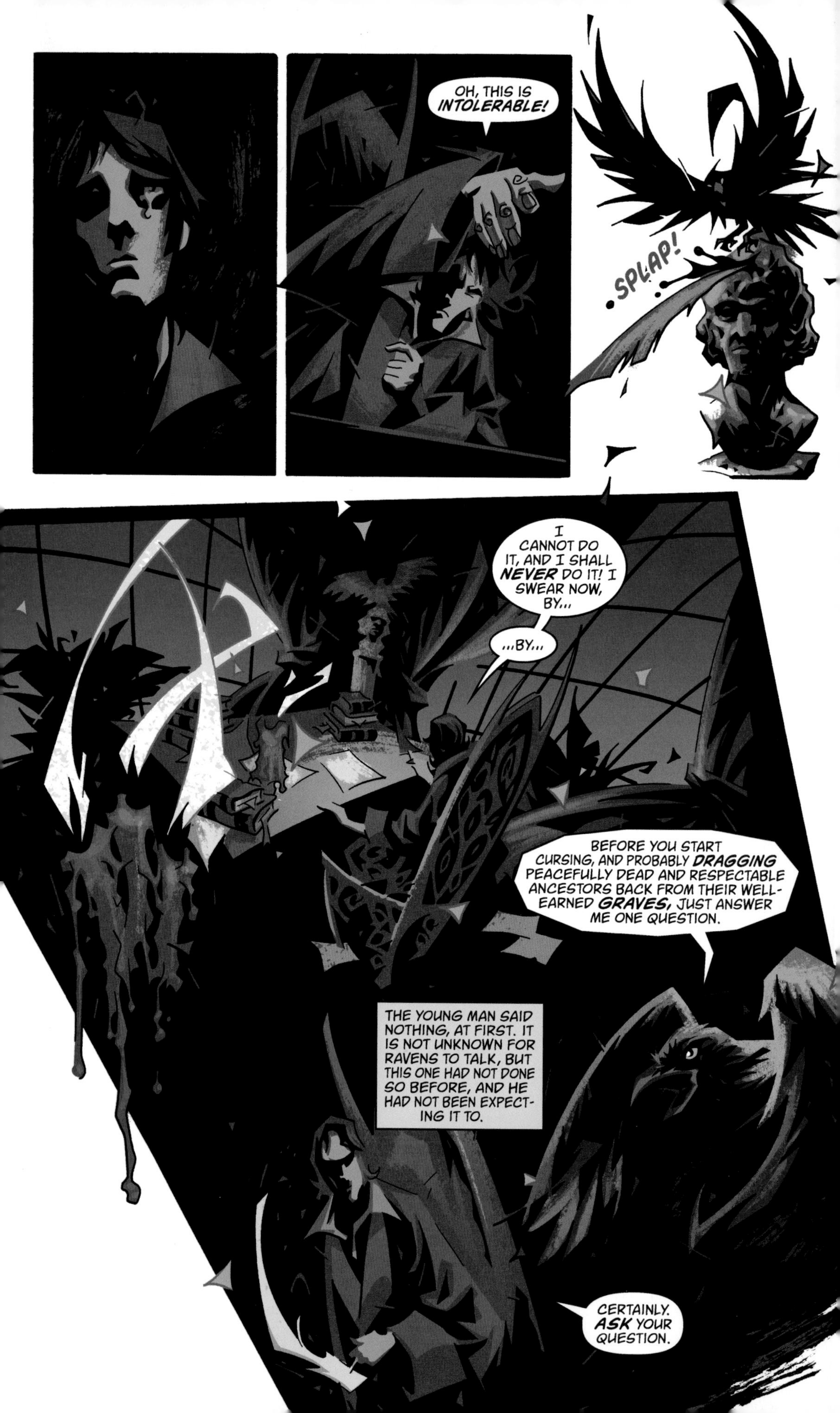

OH, THIS IS INTOLERABLE!
SPLAP!
I CANNOT DO IT, AND I SHALL NEVER DO IT! I SWEAR NOW, BY...
...BY...
BEFORE YOU START CURSING, AND PROBABLY DRAGGING PEACEFULLY DEAD AND RESPECTABLE ANCESTORS BACK FROM THEIR WELL-EARNED GRAVES, JUST ANSWER ME ONE QUESTION.
THE YOUNG MAN SAID NOTHING, AT FIRST. IT IS NOT UNKNOWN FOR RAVENS TO TALK, BUT THIS ONE HAD NOT DONE SO BEFORE, AND HE HAD NOT BEEN EXPECTING IT TO.
CERTAINLY. ASK YOUR QUESTION.

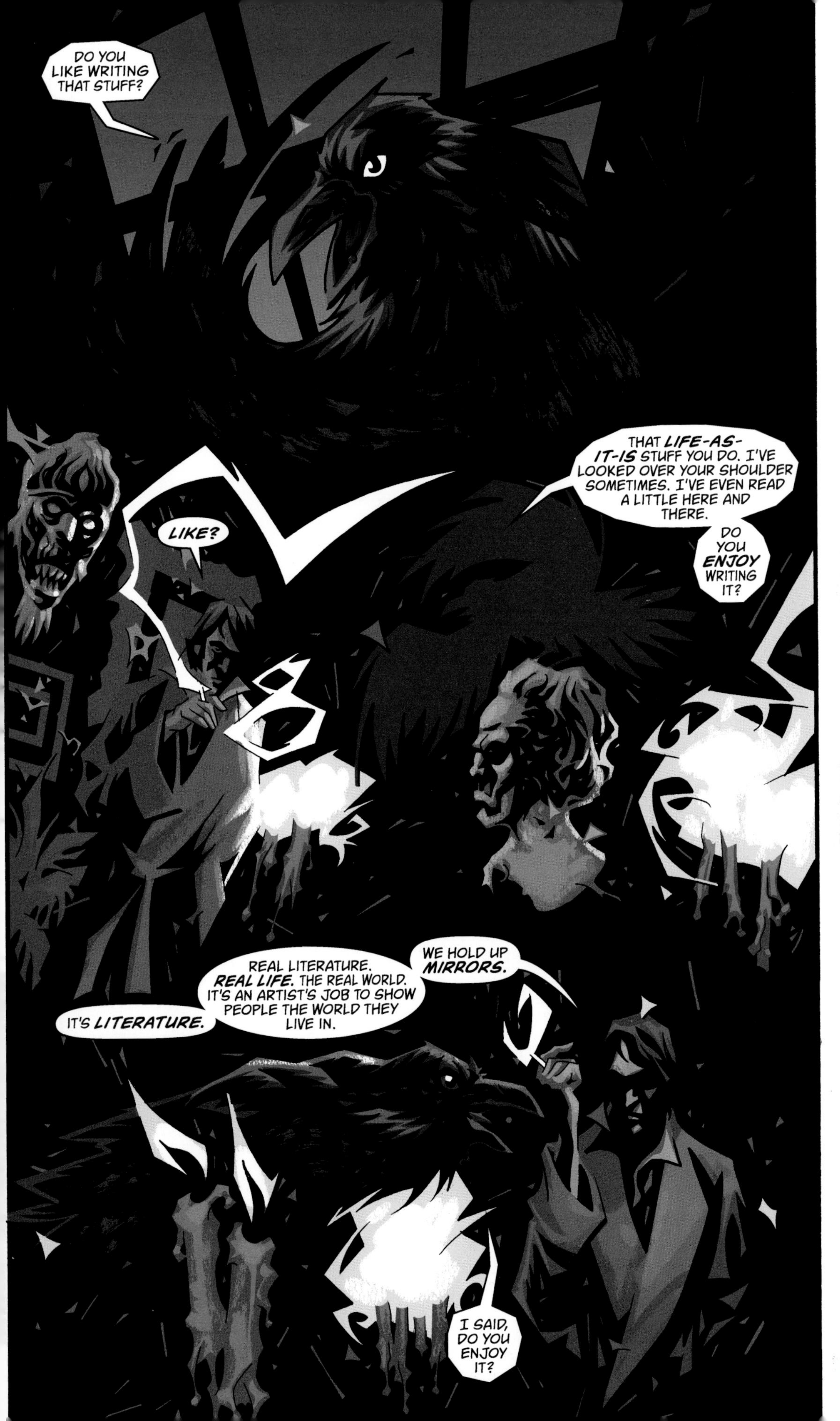
DO YOU LIKE WRITING THAT STUFF?
LIKE?
THAT LIFE-AS-IT-IS STUFF YOU DO. I'VE LOOKED OVER YOUR SHOULDER SOMETIMES. I'VE EVEN READ A LITTLE HERE AND THERE.
DO YOU ENJOY WRITING IT?
IT'S LITERATURE.
REAL LITERATURE. REAL LIFE. THE REAL WORLD. IT'S AN ARTIST'S JOB TO SHOW PEOPLE THE WORLD THEY LIVE IN.
WE HOLD UP MIRRORS.
I SAID, DO YOU ENJOY IT?

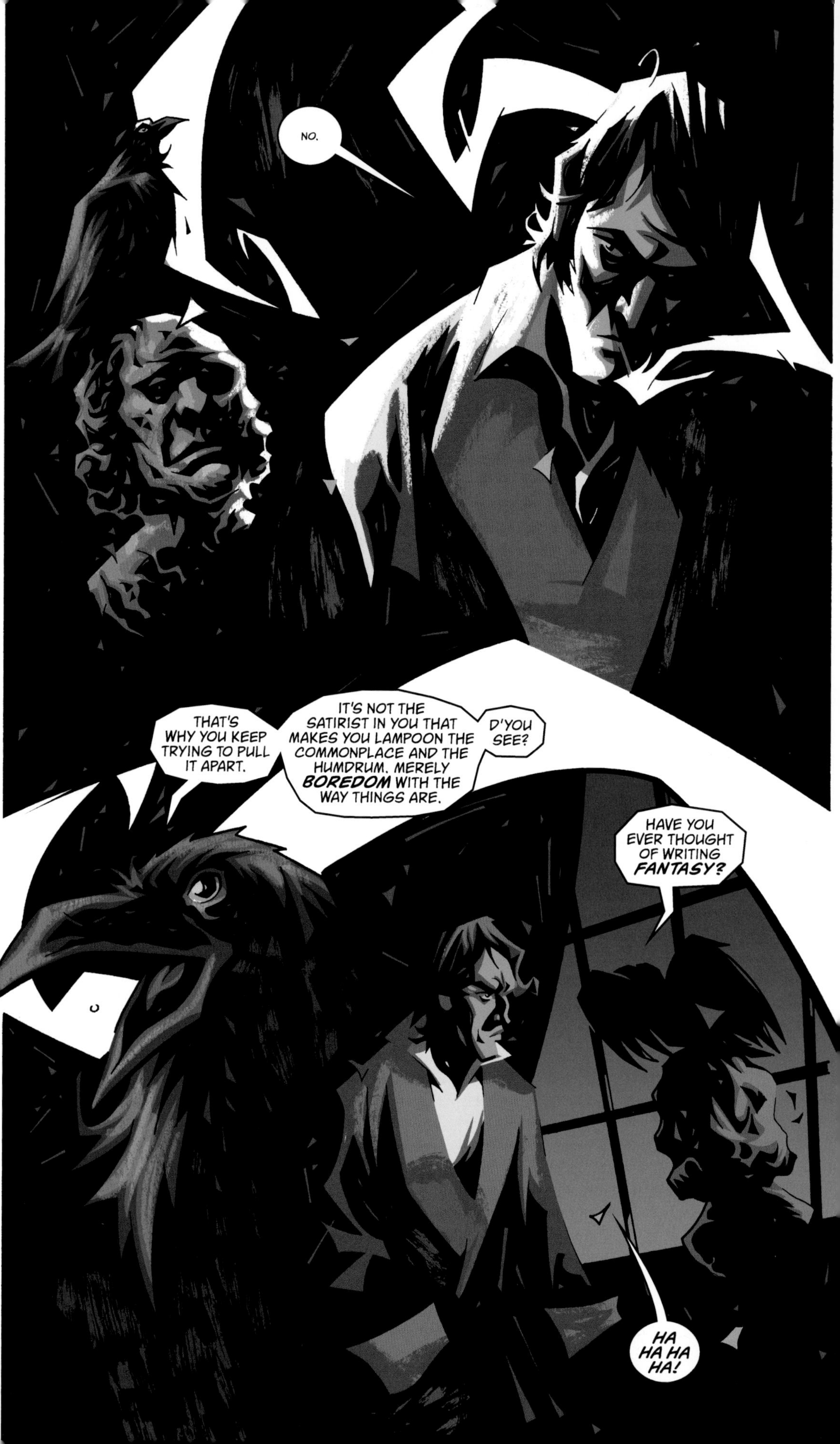
NO.
THAT'S WHY YOU KEEP TRYING TO PULL IT APART.
IT'S NOT THE SATIRIST IN YOU THAT MAKES YOU LAMPOON THE COMMONPLACE AND THE HUMDRUM. MERELY BOREDOM WITH THE WAY THINGS ARE.
D'YOU SEE?
HAVE YOU EVER THOUGHT OF WRITING FANTASY?
HA HA HA HA HA!

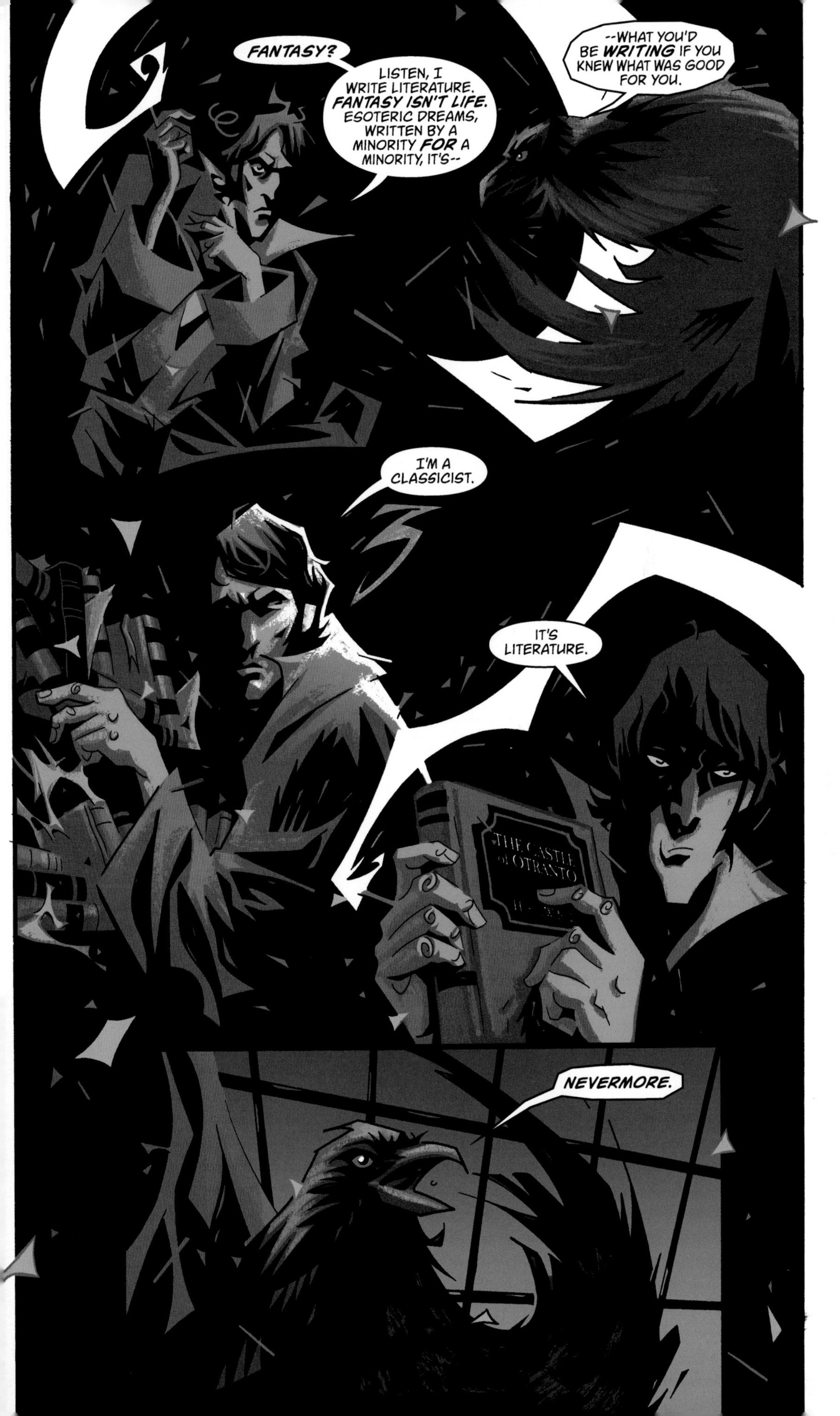
FANTASY?
LISTEN, I WRITE LITERATURE. FANTASY ISN'T LIFE. ESOTERIC DREAMS, WRITTEN BY A MINORITY FOR A MINORITY, IT'S--
--WHAT YOU'D BE WRITING IF YOU KNEW WHAT WAS GOOD FOR YOU.
I'M A CLASSICIST.
IT'S LITERATURE.
THE CASTLE of OTRANTO
NEVERMORE.

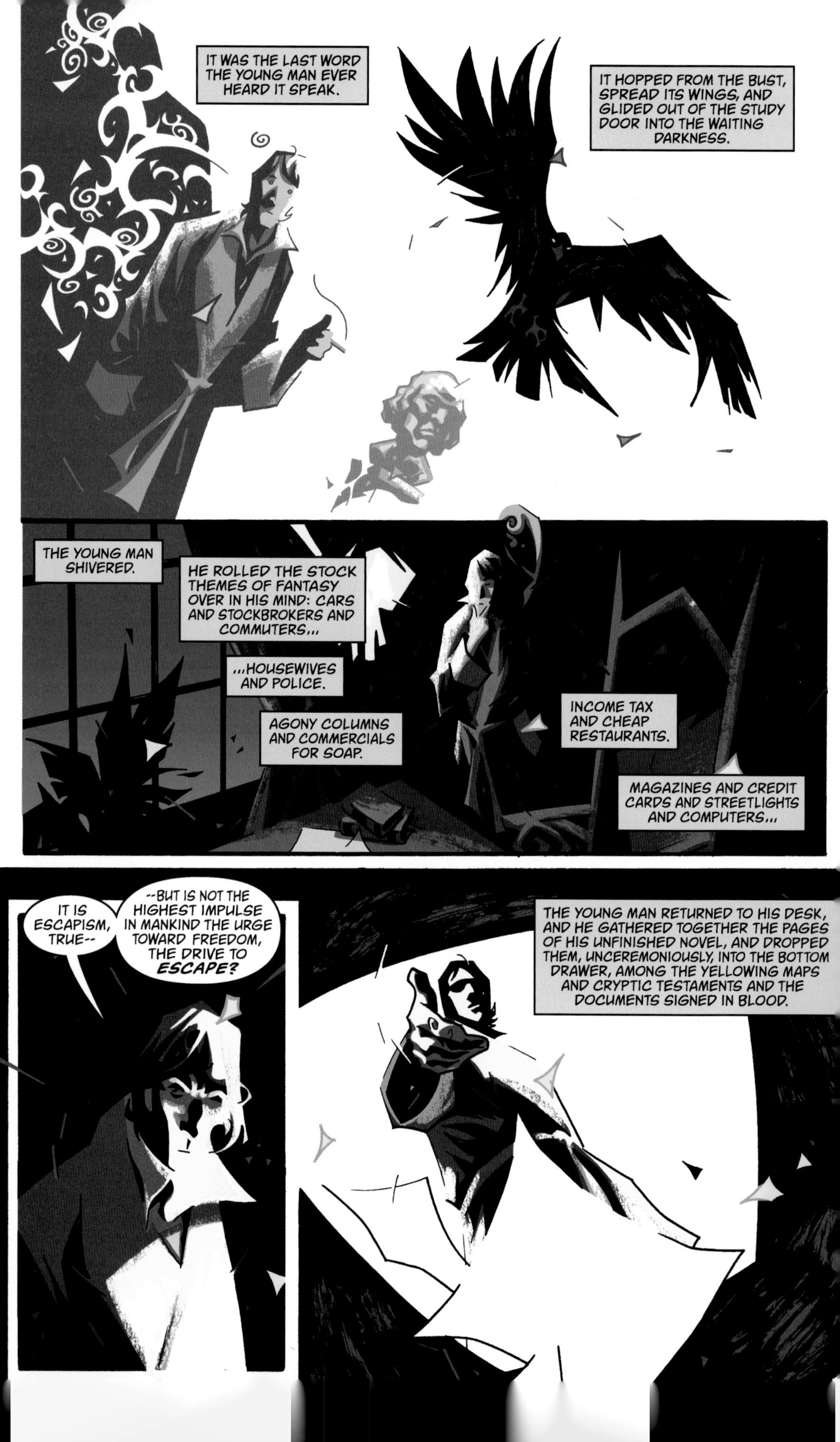

IT WAS THE LAST WORD THE YOUNG MAN EVER HEARD IT SPEAK.
IT HOPPED FROM THE BUST, SPREAD ITS WINGS, AND GLIDED OUT OF THE STUDY DOOR INTO THE WAITING DARKNESS.
THE YOUNG MAN SHIVERED.
HE ROLLED THE STOCK THEMES OF FANTASY OVER IN HIS MIND: CARS AND STOCKBROKERS AND COMMUTERS...
...HOUSEWIVES AND POLICE.
AGONY COLUMNS AND COMMERCIALS FOR SOAP.
INCOME TAX AND CHEAP RESTAURANTS.
MAGAZINES AND CREDIT CARDS AND STREETLIGHTS AND COMPUTERS...
IT IS ESCAPISM, TRUE--
--BUT IS NOT THE HIGHEST IMPULSE IN MANKIND THE URGE TOWARD FREEDOM, THE DRIVE TO ESCAPE?
THE YOUNG MAN RETURNED TO HIS DESK, AND HE GATHERED TOGETHER THE PAGES OF HIS UNFINISHED NOVEL, AND DROPPED THEM, UNCEREMONIOUSLY, INTO THE BOTTOM DRAWER, AMONG THE YELLOWING MAPS AND CRYPTIC TESTAMENTS AND THE DOCUMENTS SIGNED IN BLOOD.

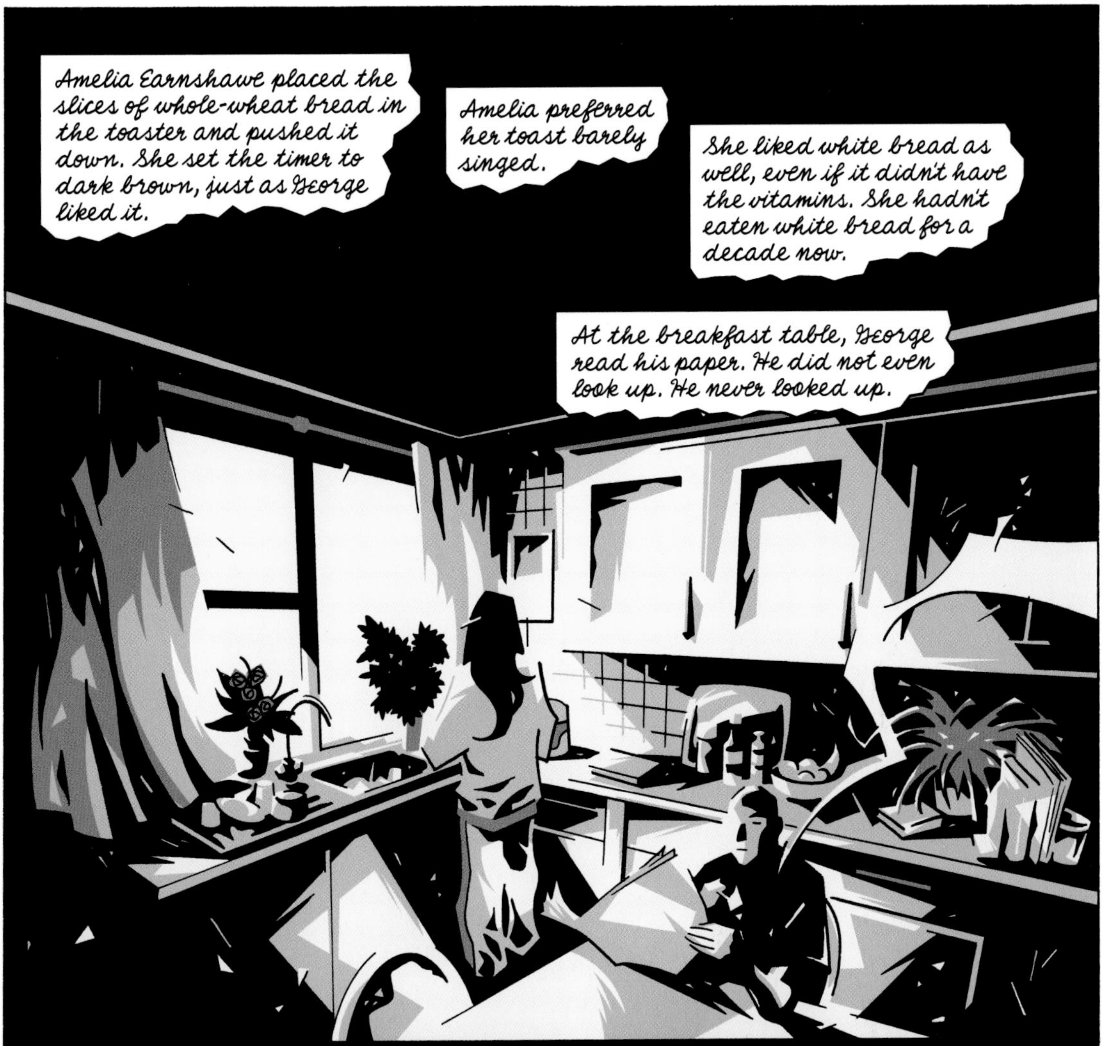
Amelia Earnshawe placed the slices of whole-wheat bread in the toaster and pushed it down. She set the timer to dark brown, just as George liked it.
Amelia preferred her toast barely singed.
She liked white bread as well, even if it didn't have the vitamins. She hadn't eaten white bread for a decade now.
At the breakfast table, George read his paper. He did not even look up. He never looked up.

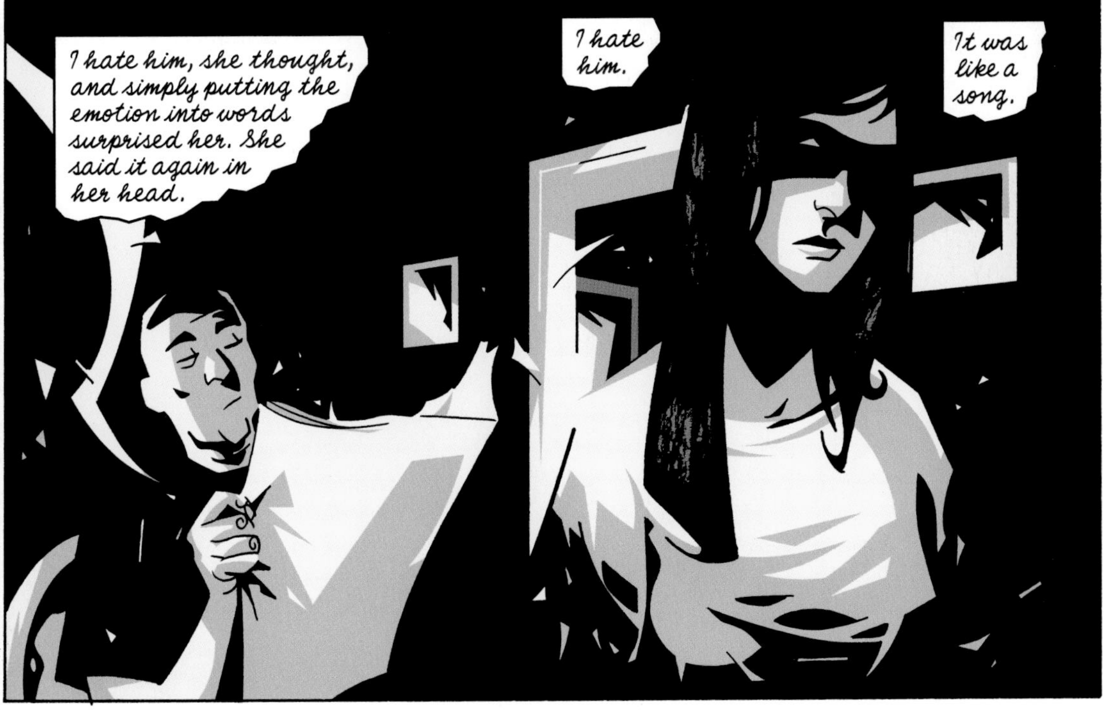
I hate him, she thought, and simply putting the emotion into words surprised her. She said it again in her head.
I hate him.
It was like a song.

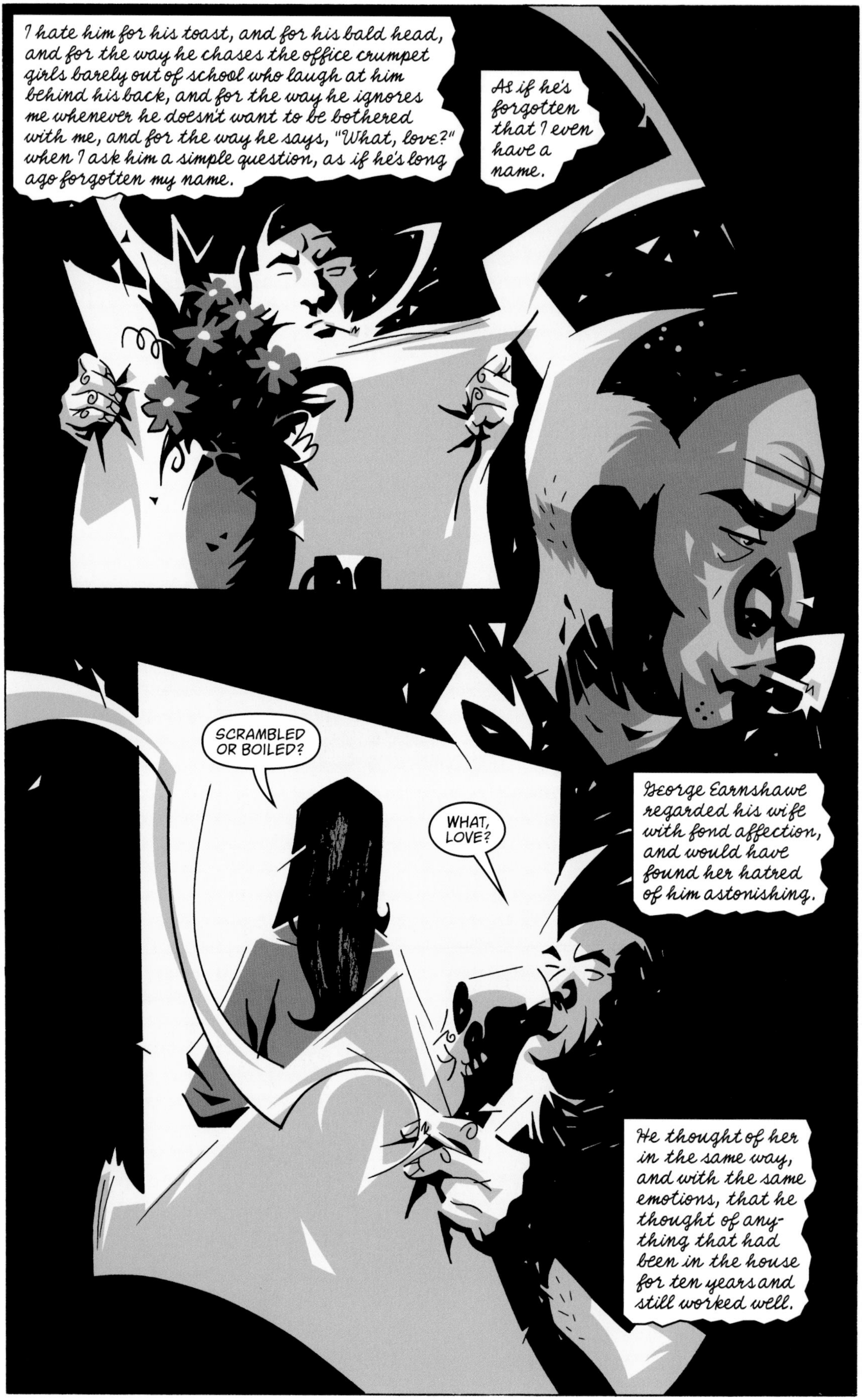
I hate him for his toast, and for his bald head, and for the way he chases the office crumpet girls barely out of school who laugh at him behind his back, and for the way he ignores me whenever he doesn't want to be bothered with me, and for the way he says, "What, love?" when I ask him a simple question, as if he's long ago forgotten my name.
As if he's forgotten that I even have a name.
SCRAMBLED OR BOILED?
WHAT, LOVE?
George Earnshawe regarded his wife with fond affection, and would have found her hatred of him astonishing.
He thought of her in the same way, and with the same emotions, that he thought of anything that had been in the house for ten years and still worked well.

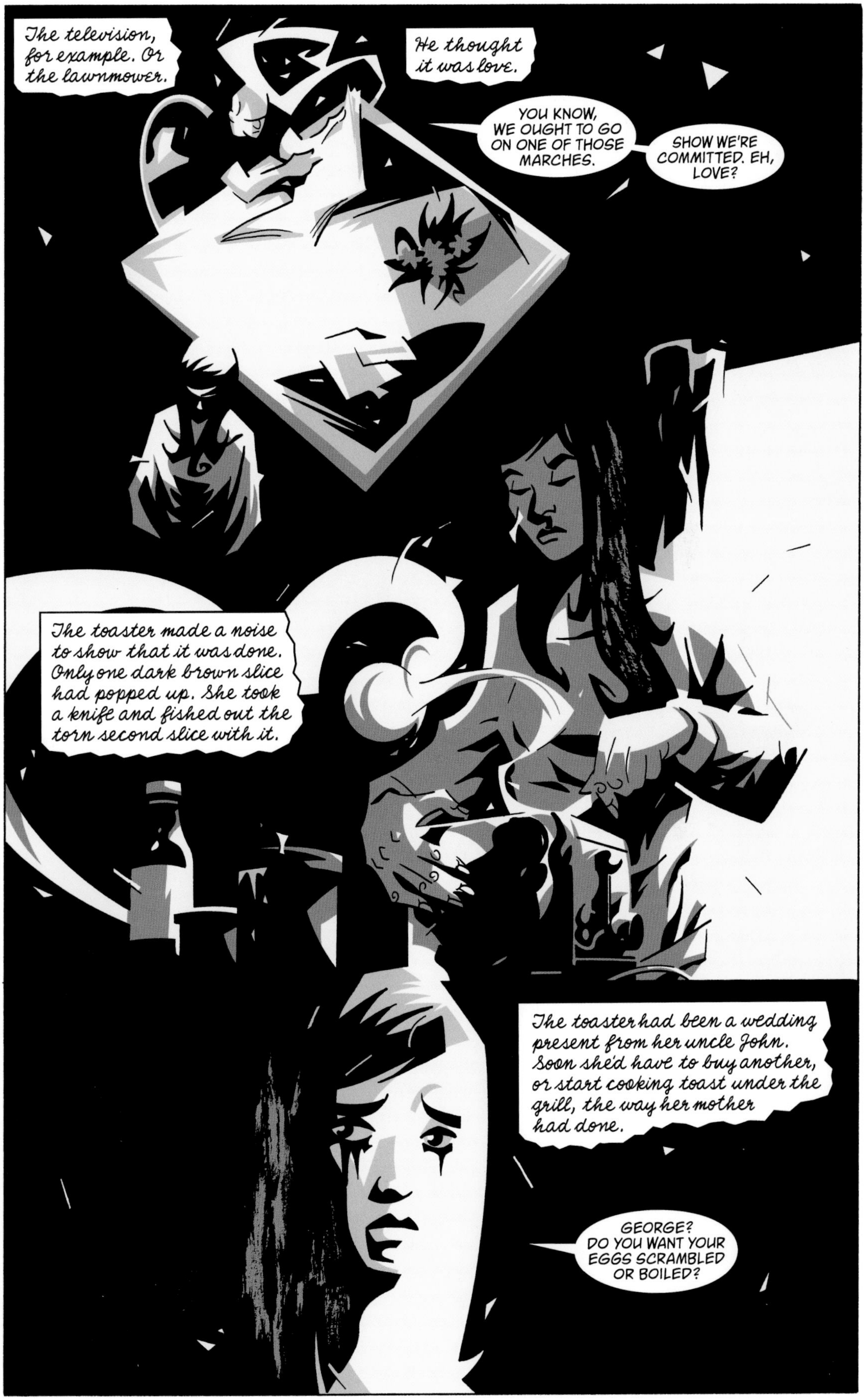
The television, for example. Or the lawnmower.
He thought it was love.
YOU KNOW, WE OUGHT TO GO ON ONE OF THOSE MARCHES.
SHOW WE'RE COMMITTED. EH, LOVE?
The toaster made a noise to show that it was done. Only one dark brown slice had popped up. She took a knife and fished out the torn second slice with it.
The toaster had been a wedding present from her uncle John. Soon she'd have to buy another, or start cooking toast under the grill, the way her mother had done.
GEORGE? DO YOU WANT YOUR EGGS SCRAMBLED OR BOILED?

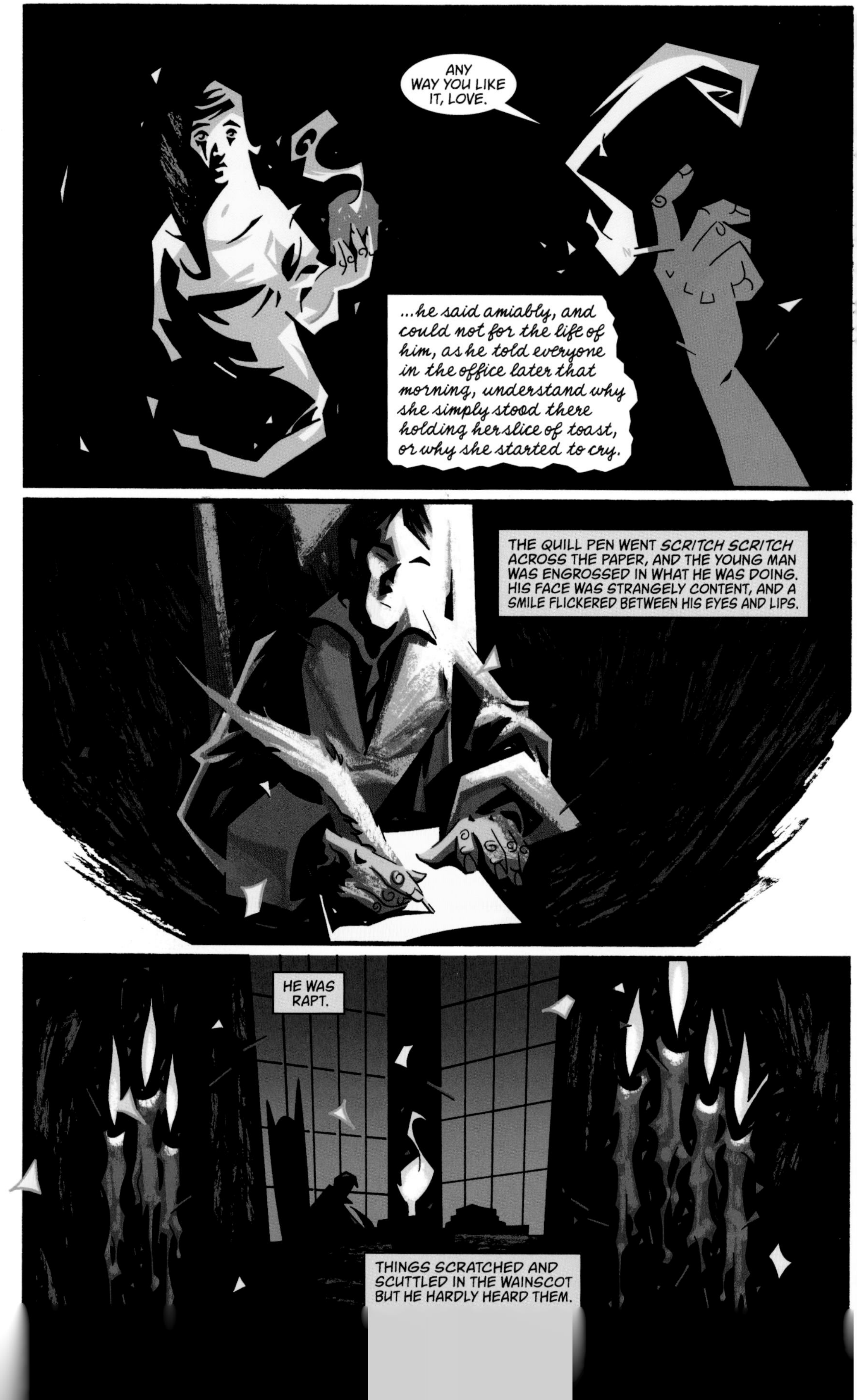

ANY WAY YOU LIKE IT, LOVE.
...he said amiably, and could not for the life of him, as he told everyone in the office later that morning, understand why she simply stood there holding her slice of toast, or why she started to cry.
THE QUILL PEN WENT *SCRITCH SCRITCH* ACROSS THE PAPER, AND THE YOUNG MAN WAS ENGROSSED IN WHAT HE WAS DOING. HIS FACE WAS STRANGELY CONTENT, AND A SMILE FLICKERED BETWEEN HIS EYES AND LIPS.
HE WAS RAPT.
THINGS SCRATCHED AND SCUTTLED IN THE WAINSCOT BUT HE HARDLY HEARD THEM.

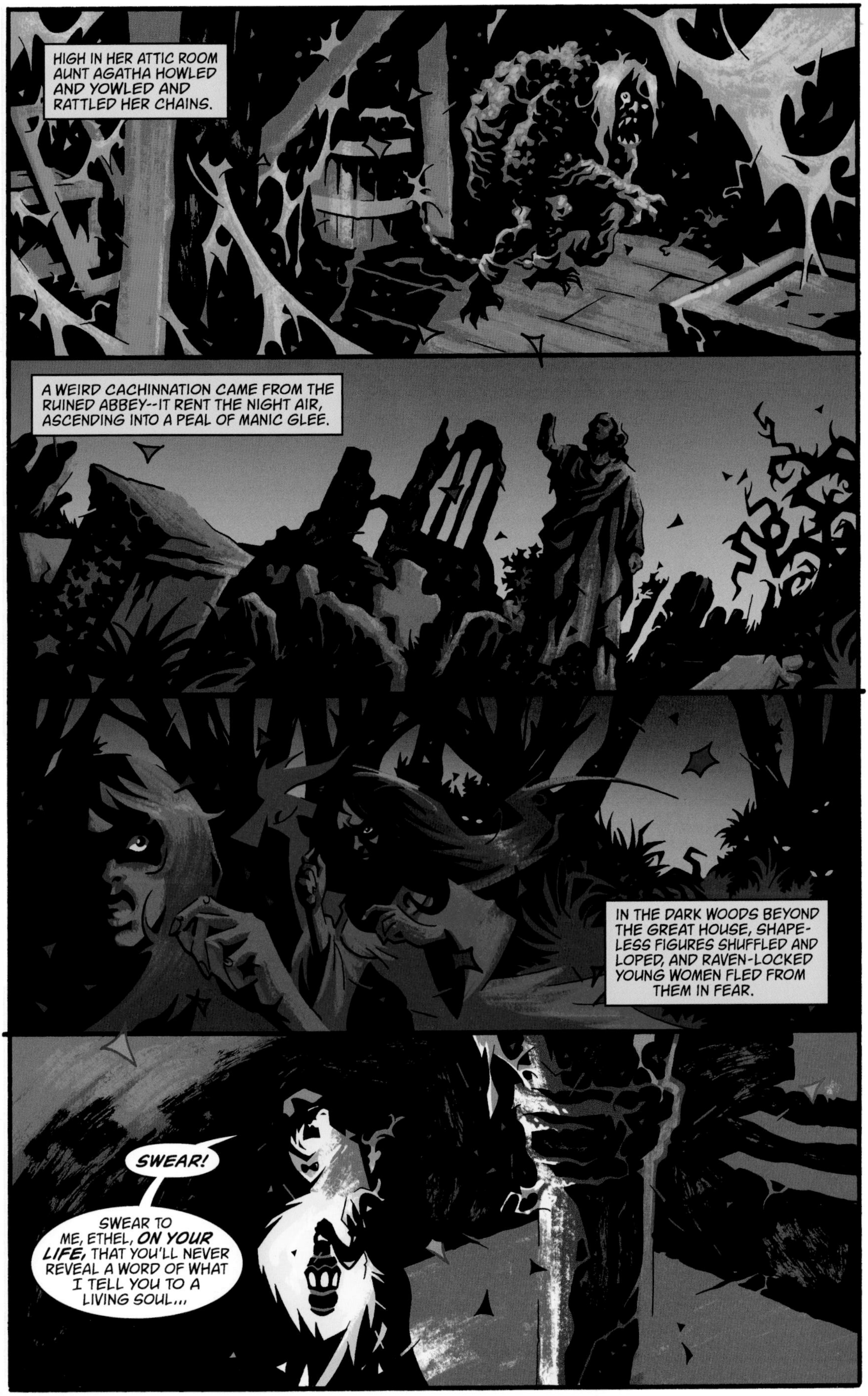
HIGH IN HER ATTIC ROOM AUNT AGATHA HOWLED AND YOWLED AND RATTLED HER CHAINS.
A WEIRD CACHINNATION CAME FROM THE RUINED ABBEY--IT RENT THE NIGHT AIR, ASCENDING INTO A PEAL OF MANIC GLEE.
IN THE DARK WOODS BEYOND THE GREAT HOUSE, SHAPE-LESS FIGURES SHUFFLED AND LOPED, AND RAVEN-LOCKED YOUNG WOMEN FLED FROM THEM IN FEAR.
SWEAR!
SWEAR TO ME, ETHEL, ON YOUR LIFE, THAT YOU'LL NEVER REVEAL A WORD OF WHAT I TELL YOU TO A LIVING SOUL...

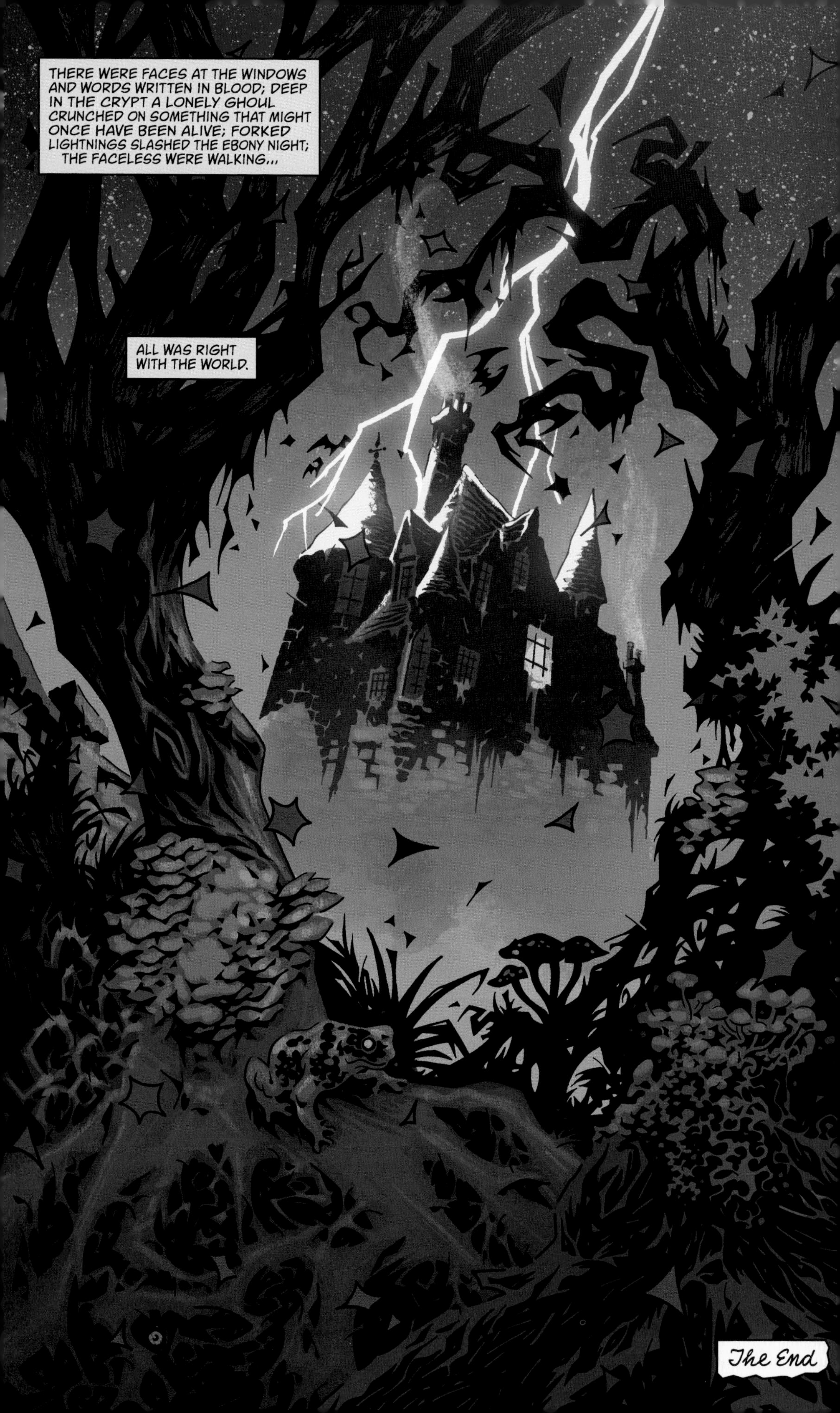
THERE WERE FACES AT THE WINDOWS AND WORDS WRITTEN IN BLOOD; DEEP IN THE CRYPT A LONELY GHOUL CRUNCHED ON SOMETHING THAT MIGHT ONCE HAVE BEEN ALIVE; FORKED LIGHTNINGS SLASHED THE EBONY NIGHT; THE FACELESS WERE WALKING...
ALL WAS RIGHT WITH THE WORLD.
The End

FORBIDDEN BRIDES

SKETCHBOOK

NOTES BY SHANE OAKLEY

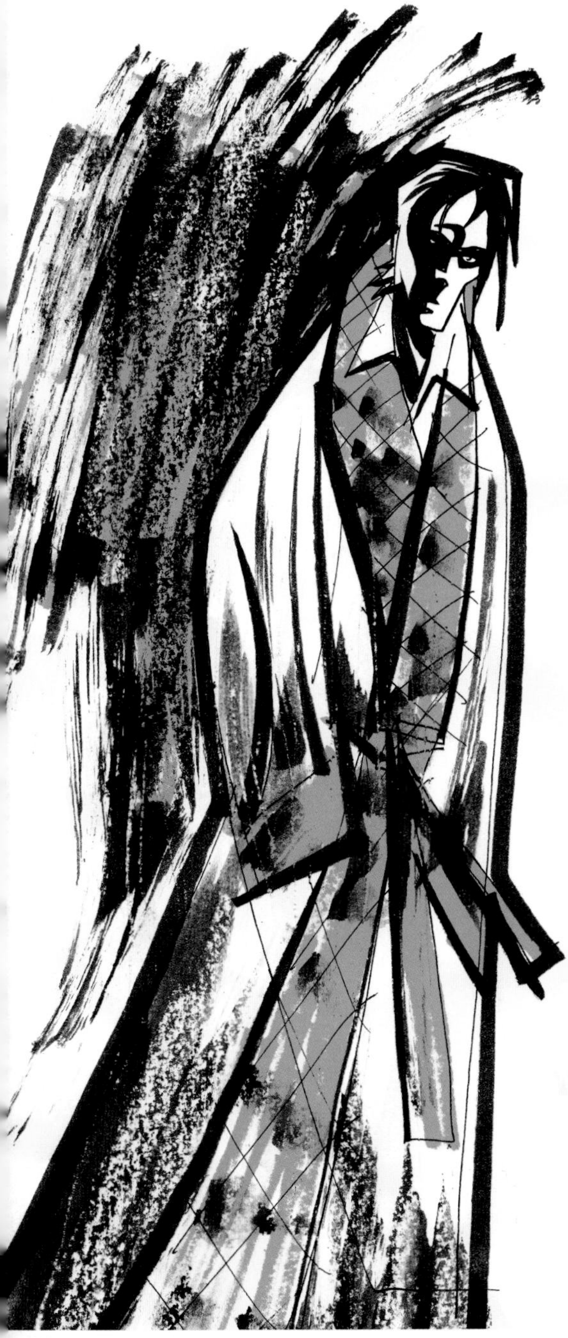

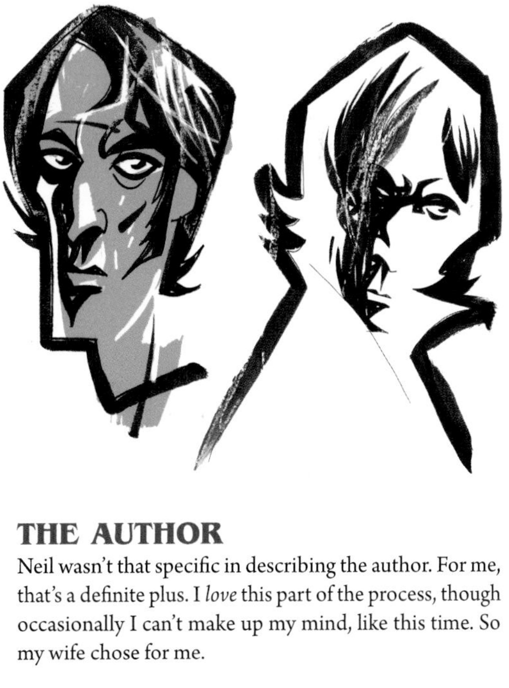

THE AUTHOR

Neil wasn't that specific in describing the author. For me, that's a definite plus. I *love* this part of the process, though occasionally I can't make up my mind, like this time. So my wife chose for me.

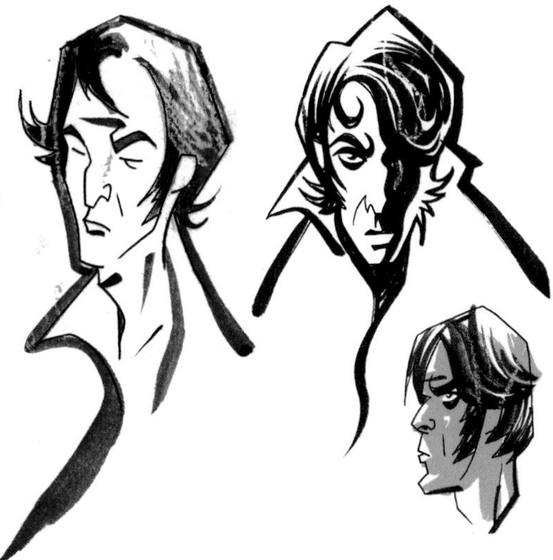

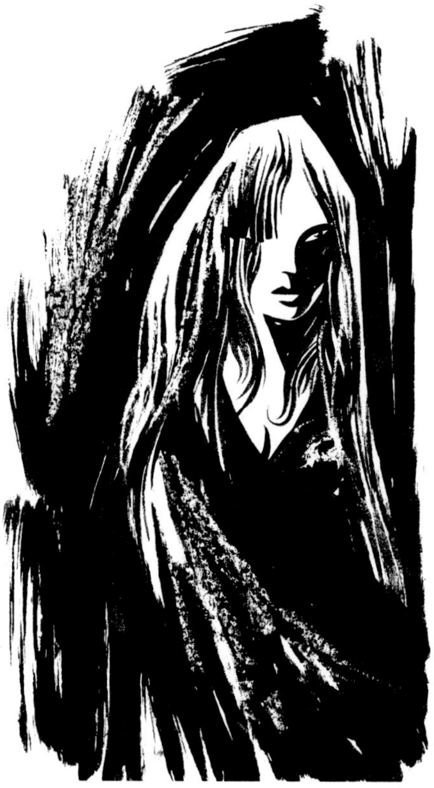

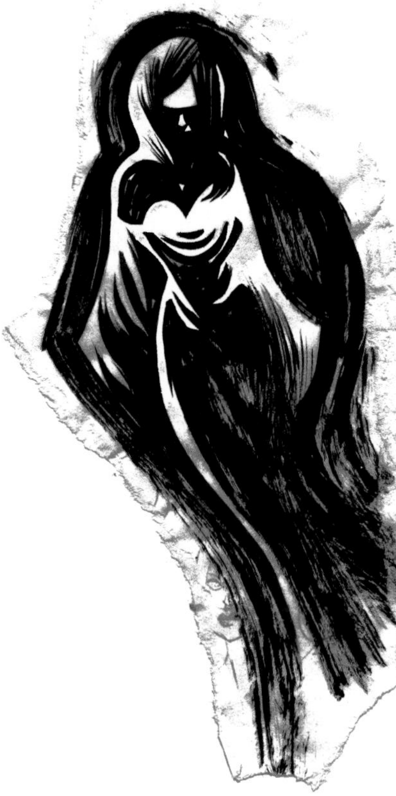

AMELIA

Amelia is pretty much your archetypal wary woman on a gothic romance paperback book cover. And I was also picturing various B- and C-list starlets from Hammer vampire movies.

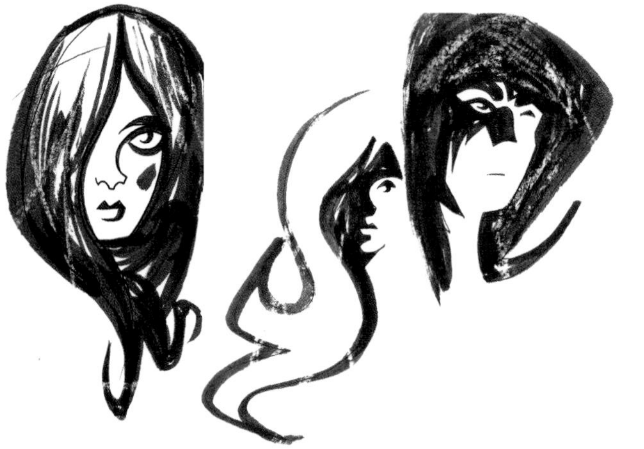

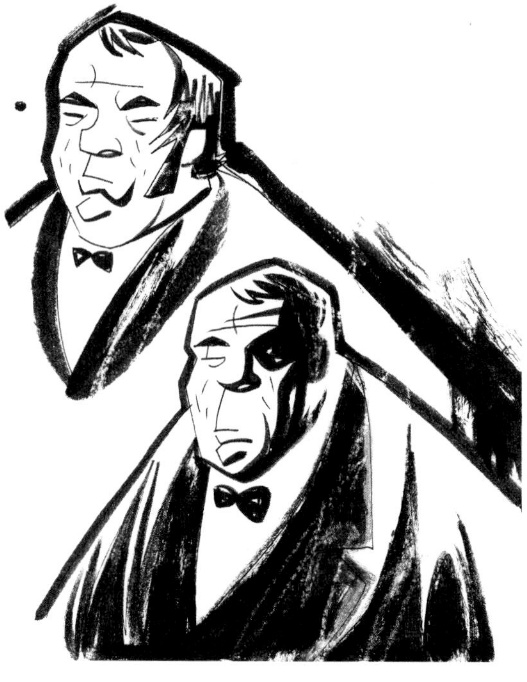

THE BUTLER

Originally based on English actor Geoffrey Palmer. All condescending brows and bloodhound jowls. Ended up looking like Richard Nixon. Never a good thing. Dropped that idea.

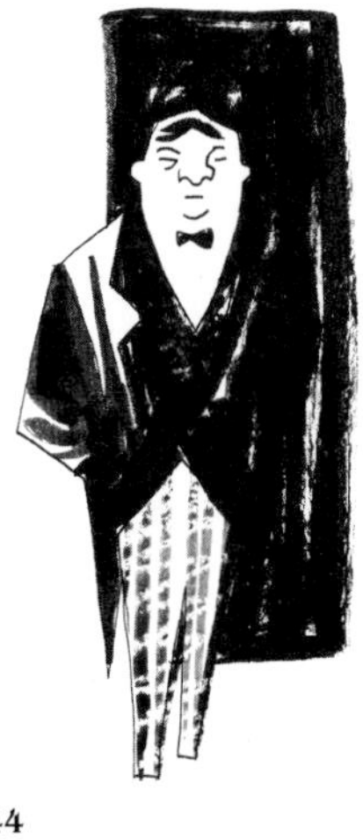

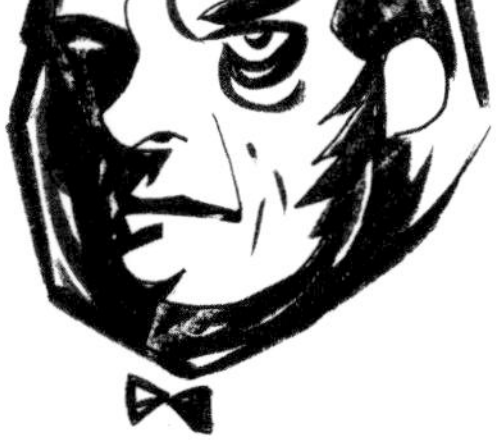

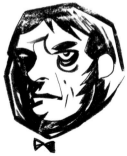

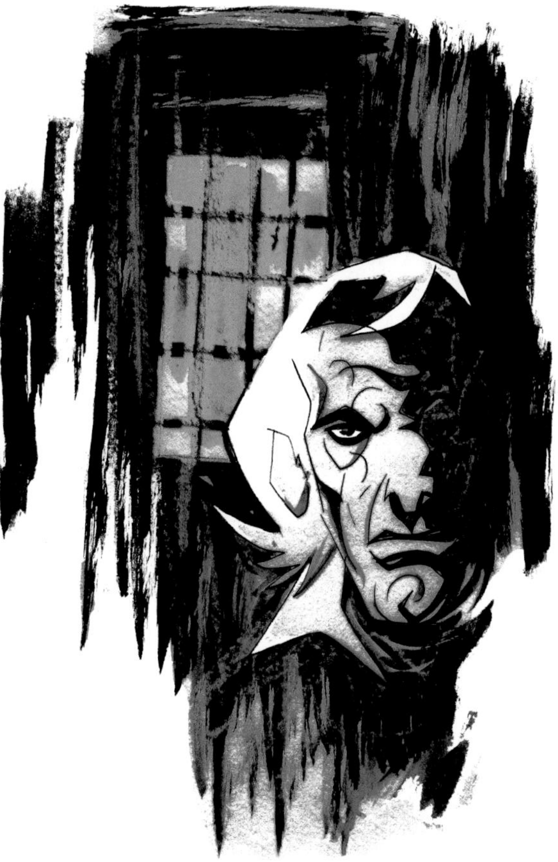

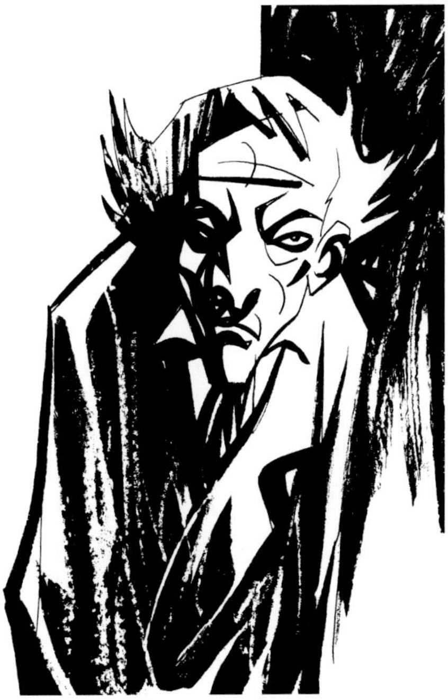

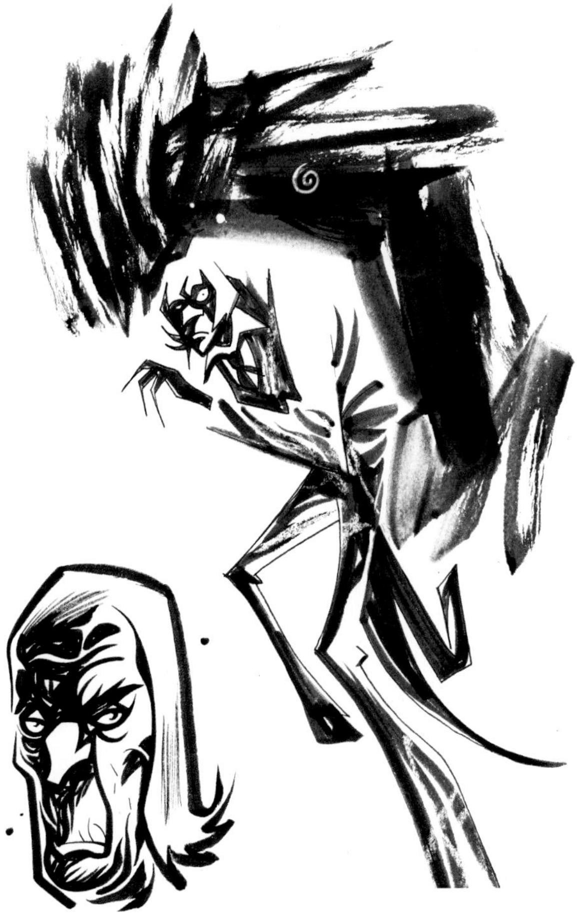

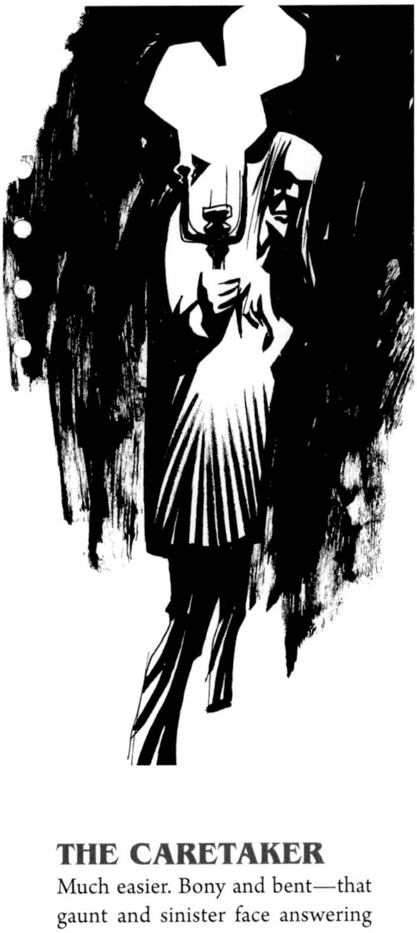

THE CARETAKER

Much easier. Bony and bent—that gaunt and sinister face answering many a door at midnight. Squint, and it's almost Uncle Creepy.

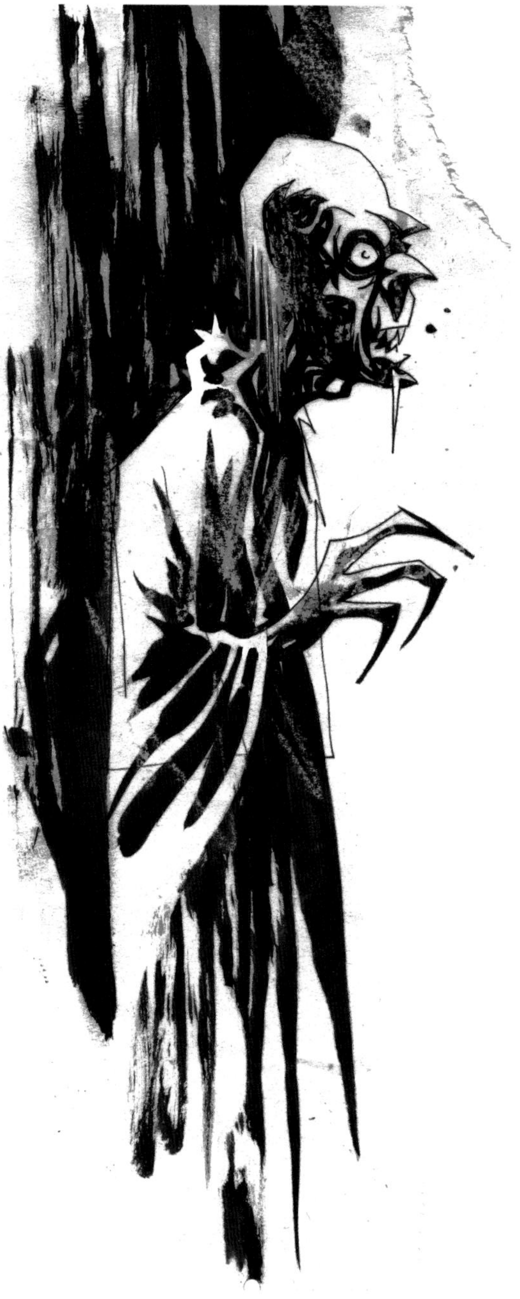

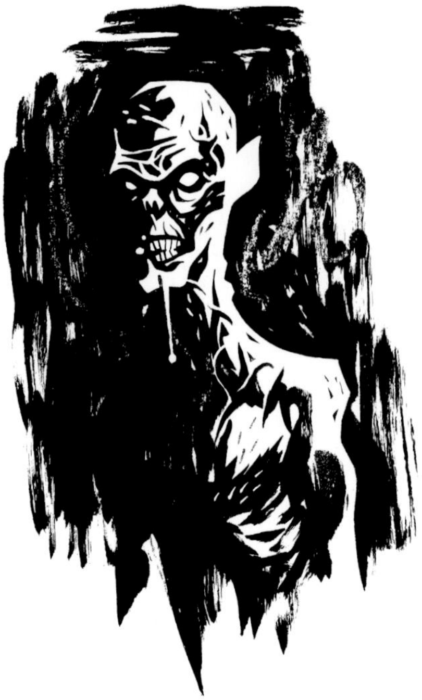

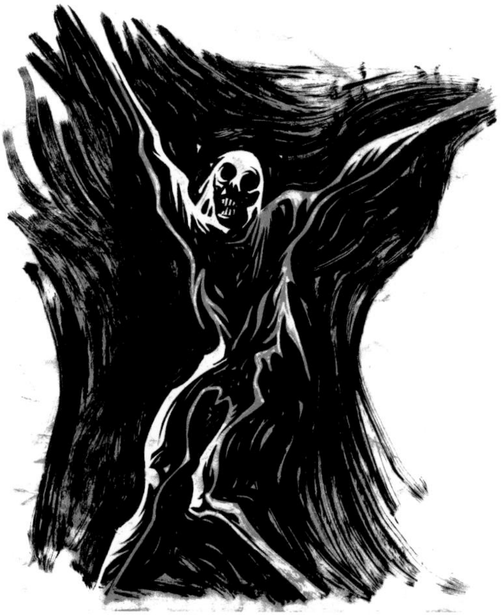

THE GHOULS

I could've filled this book with ghoul sketches. Indulged myself way too much. I even gave them names and pondered their origins and day-to-day lifestyle. Why were some dressed in monk robes? Where were the girl ghouls?

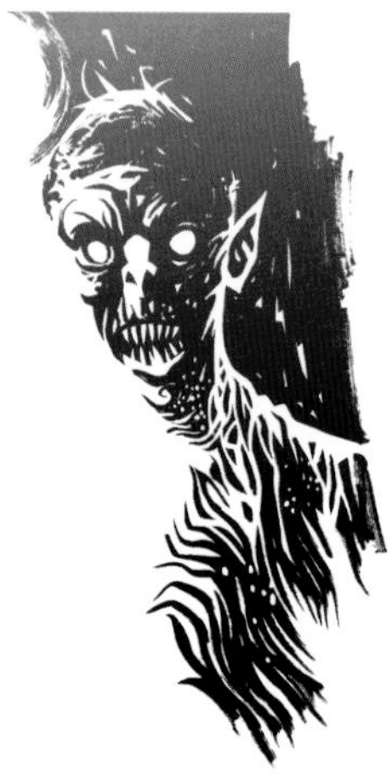

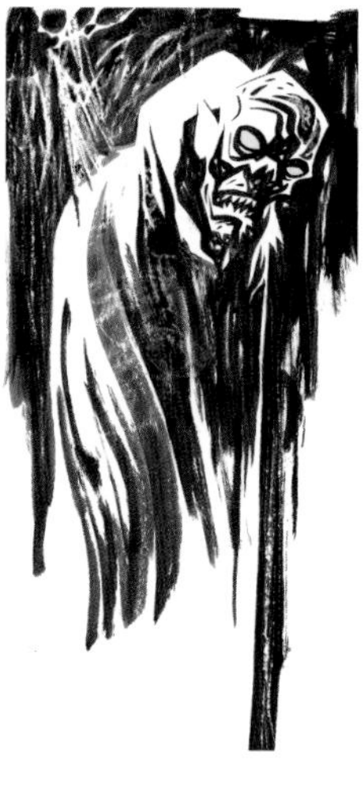

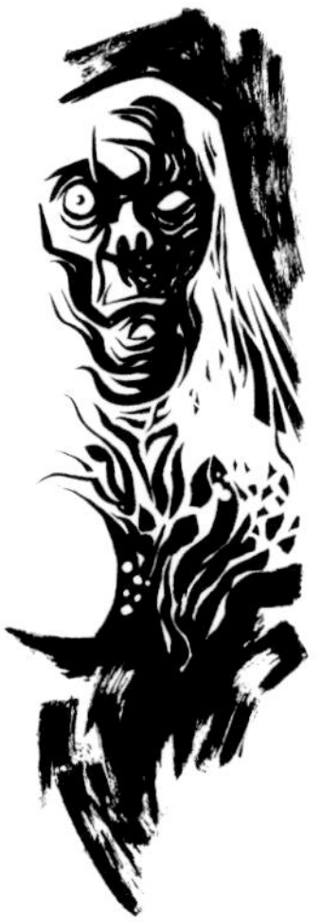

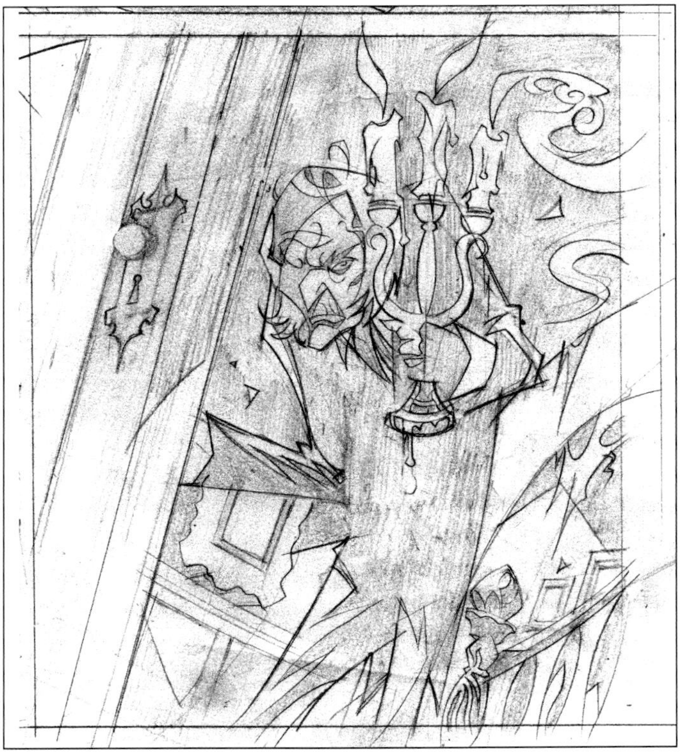

UNUSED PANEL

It was a good panel, but I don't think it had enough impact. Not for the reveal. Kick myself I forgot to use the pose further on.

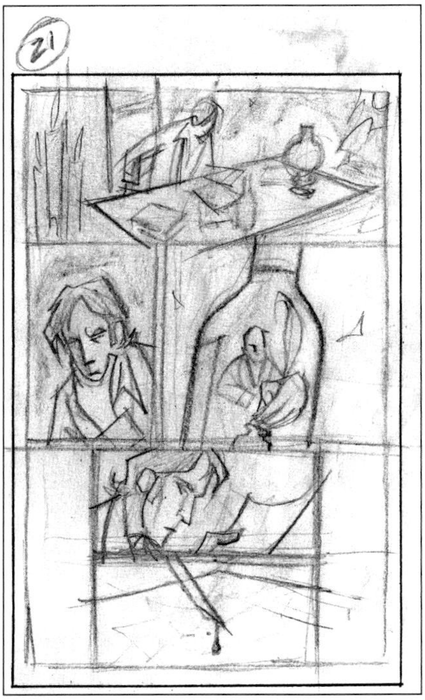

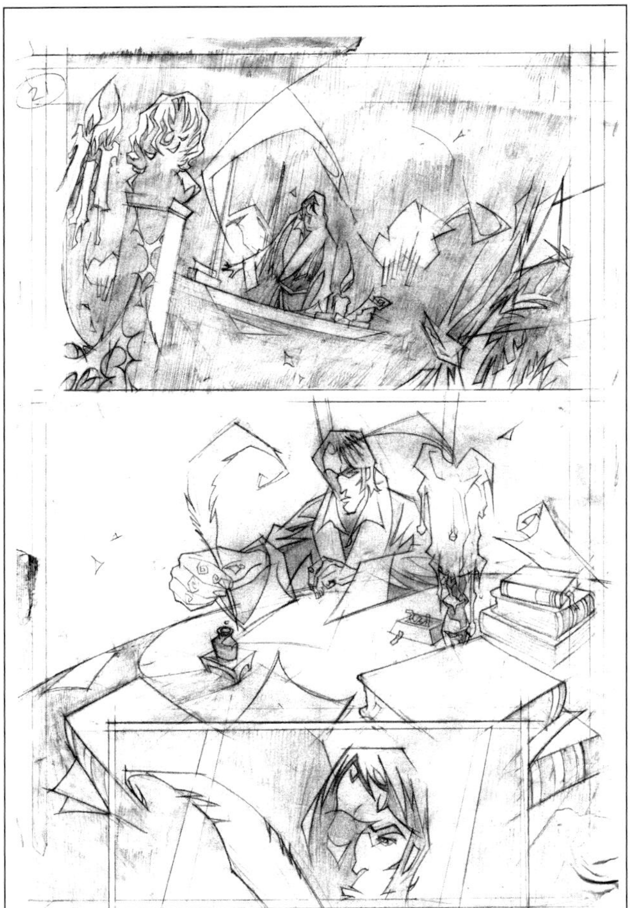

LAYOUTS VS. FINISHED PENCILS

Usually I follow my thumbnails closely, but the page needed less fuss and more drama. I also decided he wouldn't drink wine on the job (perhaps preferring an opium pipe). See, me overthinking it again.

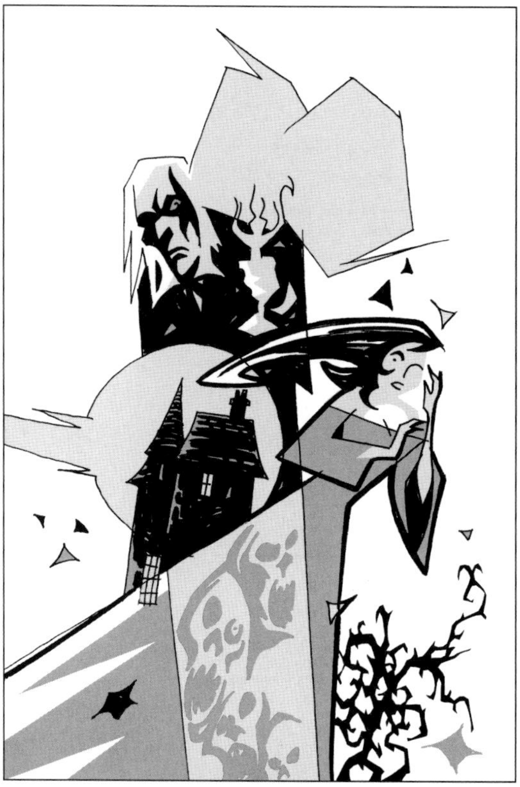

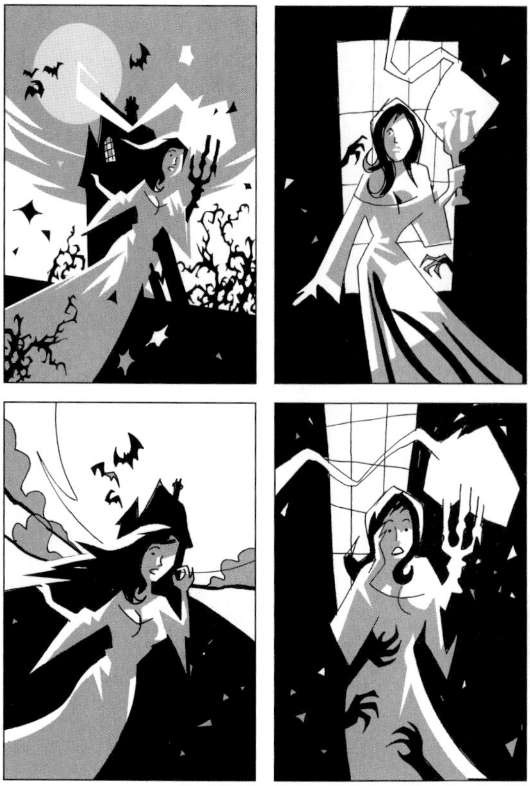

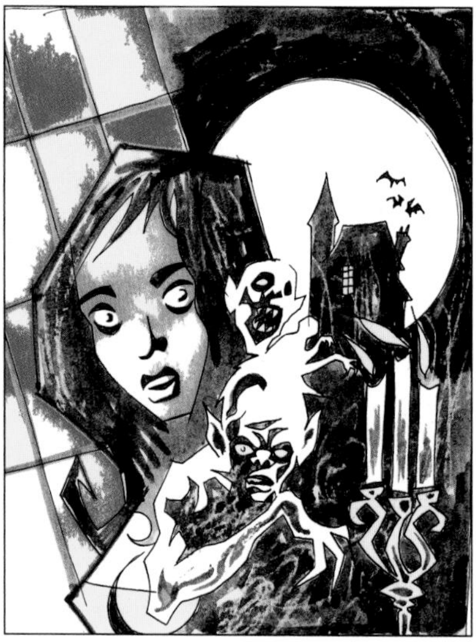

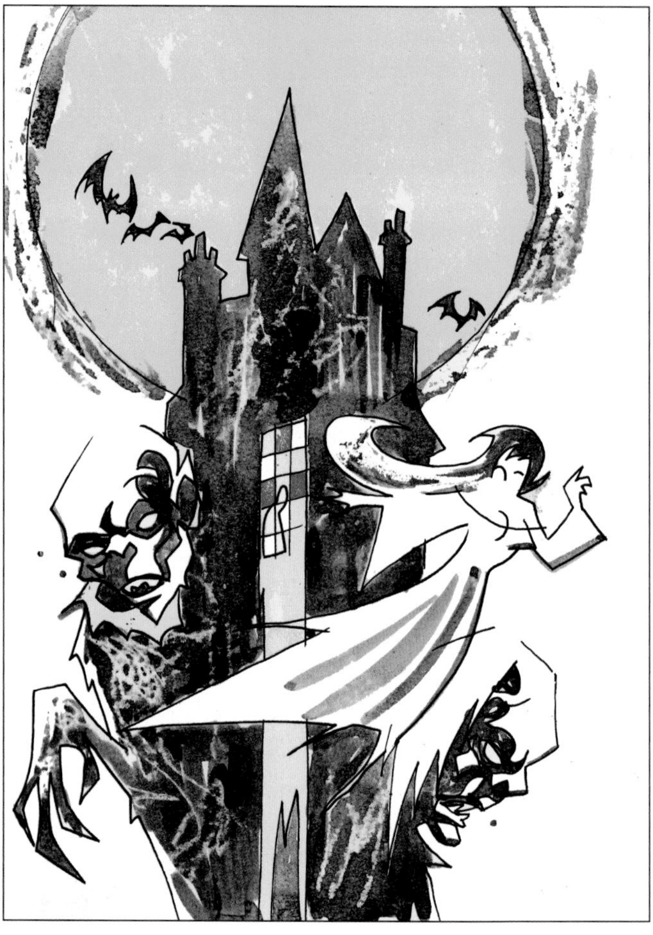

COVER

The cover was the toughest I've done. I wanted the composition to be as simple as possible, but choosing what to put in and leave out proved a major headache. So many, many variables. Wife helped again.